THE VOICE OF THE FATHER

The Voice of The Father

Learning to Listen to God in Everyday Life

Tracy Williamson

Hodder & Stoughton
LONDON SYDNEY AUCKLAND

First published in Great Britain 1996

10 9 8 7 6 5 4 3 2 1

British Library Cataloguing in Publication Data
A record for this book is available from the British Library

ISBN 0 340 63014 0

Printed and bound in Great Britain by

Cox & Wyman Ltd, Reading, Berks.

Hodder and Stoughton Ltd
A Division of Hodder Headline PLC
338 Euston Road
London NW1 3BH

For John and Amanda who showed me so much of the love of God when I first became a Christian

And for my nephews, Lee and Michael, in the hope that one day, they may hear the loving voice of the Father for themselves.

Contents

Acknowledgments

There are so many people I would like to thank it is impossible to name them all. I must begin with Bill Stanton who some years ago responded to my desire to express myself in writing and through his consultancy 'Writers' Tutorial' taught me so much. His persevering and wise encouragement despite my many mistakes gave me the courage to undertake the writing of this book. Thank you Bill for helping to make my desire actuality.

Over the fifteen months it has taken for this book to come together, countless people have contributed in different ways. Here are just a few but I am grateful to you all.

First of all, I must thank the army of friends and prayer partners who have stood with me through this time, praying so positively for each chapter, and those special people who responded to my panicky phone calls.

Thank you to Judith, Anne, Debra, Penny, Bela, SP, Lorraine and Mum – my lovely close friends and family who put up so willingly with the many months of me being too busy or absorbed with the book to spend much time with them. Thank you to each person who has given permission for your name and story to be used in the book. I am so grateful and I know the stories really bring the book alive. Thank you too, to the many people who have contributed without realising it, the challenging stories I've taken from other books, the different people I've met in our concerts and those who unknowingly have inspired and taught me so much about listening to God.

Thank you to David, my first pastor who has now died, and his wife Daphne. He showed me the Father heart of God. Thank you to Carolyn Armitage who gave me such encouragement at the very beginning of the book's life and to my editor, Elspeth Taylor.

Very special thanks to Jennifer Rees Larcombe whose idea it was that I should write this book in the first place. Despite her very busy lifestyle she has been such a source of help and support. Thank you, Jen.

Most of all, thank you so much, Marilyn, for being such a wonderful friend and inspiration to me. Thank you for the sacrifices you made so I could spend time on the book. Thank you for teaching me so much from your own life about listening to God and thank you for trusting me, when I first joined you, to step out in the things I believed God was showing me.

Finally, a huge thank you from the bottom of my heart to my Father God for without Him this book could never have been written.

Tracy Williamson

NB: For the sake of confidentiality I have sometimes given people different names.

Introduction

I have known Tracy for over ten years now and count it a very great privilege having her work alongside me. Not only is she a tremendous help, but over the years she has become a very dear friend.

Her enthusiasm for listening to God has certainly rubbed off on me! I longed to hear him, and I did at times, but it seemed spasmodic and dependent on the mood of the moment.

When people came up to us at the end of a concert, expressing their deep needs and asking for a prayer, I began to realise how very important listening to God could be. Often Tracy would not hear what they were saying in the hubbub, especially if they were distressed. But time and time again, the Lord would give her something just right for that person. The fact that she had not heard the conversation but still came up with something so illuminating, only added to the conviction that God Himself was stepping in, bringing special help into the situation.

So when she did her first workshops on hearing God in everyday life, a new longing to hear Him much more consistently began to take root in my own heart. I began to try to make it a priority to hear Him everyday. I used to think it was because Tracy is deaf that she had a special 'hot-line' to Jesus, but as I put into practice some of the things she was suggesting and believed He wanted to communicate with me just as much as He did with her, I began to experience new depths of intimacy with Him.

Tracy's longing to hear God and her love for Him has been a

real means of inspiration to me, so that drawing close to God and hearing His voice has become the most important thing in my life. Thank you, Tracy, for all you have taught me, I can never thank you enough.

Marilyn Baker

Foreword

Through many years of illness and frequent hospitalisation I was helped and comforted many times over as I listened to Marilyn Baker tapes. So I was most excited as I set off to hear her 'live' for the very first time. I took a friend with me who had not been a Christian very long. We both loved it and the music just wrapped round us like warm treacle. We noticed Tracy sitting near Marilyn on the stage and assumed she was there to guide Marilyn to and from the mike and find things she might lose or need. However, towards the end of the concert Tracy came to the microphone herself and said, 'I can see a picture of a child's party dress. It's made of pink lace with white ribbons and little satin roses round the collar. I think God wants to give it to someone here to show them how much he loves them. They have never been able to believe He loves them because their own father never did.' At this my friend dissolved into tears and told me later, 'I knew that picture was for me, because my father always favoured my sister – she was pretty and clever and Daddy's girl. He hardly seemed to notice me. Once, when she was invited to a friend's party he bought her a dress *exactly* like the one Tracy described and, at the time, I felt gutted. I'd forgotten all about it, but since I became a Christian I've really struggled with the feeling that God could ever love me. I guess I feel He must love other, more attractive Christians far more – just like my Dad loved my sister best.'

The whole evening blessed my friend so much that my husband and I plucked up the courage to ask Marilyn and Tracy to help us run one of our Hildenborougn Holidays the following summer. They kindly agreed and we met to plan and pray together about it a few months before the event. It was then that I realised how limited Tracy's hearing really is. She was unable to join in our discussion because she simply could not hear what we were saying. Yet towards the end she suddenly said, 'I feel God is saying there's going to be someone coming away with us who has an eating problem and He wants to bless them and give them their heart's desire.' We all agreed to pray for this nameless person, and over the following months we did so. I have to admit I eyed all our guests speculatively as they arrived but none of them looked as if they had an eating problem – perhaps Tracy had got it wrong? Then towards the end of the week a girl came to talk to me. She had brought her mother away on the holiday because she was not yet a Christian. 'Mum isn't enjoying it much,' she told me sadly. 'And my greatest desire is that she might find the Lord for herself.'

'Have *you* enjoyed the week?' I ventured.

'Well . . . you see, I have this eating problem . . .'

Without thinking I exclaimed, 'Oh, *you* must be the person we've been praying for all these months.'

She flushed scarlet and said, 'Oh no! No one knows about my problems, no one at all.'

'God does,' I said gently, 'and He cares so much about it that He's had us all praying for you.' She was so overcome by the caring love of the Lord that she told her mother all about it. She, in her turn, was so amazed that on the last night of the holiday she gave her life to the Lord and has followed Him ever since.

Since then I have often sat with Tracy while she has been praying with people, and the gift the Lord has given her never ceases to amaze me. She often cannot hear one word of all the sad stories they pour out in their distress, but they do not realise that as she sits there nodding and smiling encouragement. Then suddenly she will come out with something which cuts gently and lovingly to the very heart of the person's problem. No one is ever offended because it is obvious that no human knowledge or skill is involved. It just has to be God Himself speaking to them through Tracy. I too have been on the receiving end of her ministry and found her insights to be life-changing.

'What a gift God has given you,' I told her one day when we were running another Hildenborough Holiday together.

'But anyone can hear God,' she replied. 'He's a loving Father who longs to communicate with His children. The trouble is that most of us never learn the skill of listening to Him.' Before Tracy really knew what was happening she found she had 'volunteered' to run a workshop on listening to God the following day.

Most of the members of the house party turned up for it, eager to know 'Tracy's secret'. Many had never realised how God speaks to ordinary, everyday people through ordinary, everyday things. None of us who attended that workshop has ever been quite the same since. So I suggested that she should share her vision for listening to God with a wider group of Christians by writing this book. I know you will enjoy it, but I also know that reading it could change your life!

Jennifer Rees Larcombe

Prologue

'Would you like to meet Marilyn Baker?'

Marilyn Baker . . . immediately my mind flew back to a night several months before. Some of my friends from church had tickets to go to a concert of blind singer/songwriter Marilyn Baker. There was a spare ticket, would I like to go?

That night I had been bathed in God's love as Marilyn sang and ministered. Here was someone who could truly communicate the heart of God.

'Yes, I would love to meet her,' I answered.

Five months later Marilyn's assistant decided to leave. I was unemployed and waiting for a course to begin so Marilyn asked if I could help her out temporarily.

In January 1986, we went to our first concert together. Before it began, Marilyn asked me to pray and see if there was anything the Lord wanted to show us for the evening. This was the first time I had tried to listen to the Lord for things to say to other people and I was amazed and excited when specific ideas and verses came to my mind which, when I told Marilyn, tallied with her own.

That night, when I gave my testimony the words came with a depth and fluency that I knew only God could have given me. Later I shared the thoughts the Lord had given me and I saw that people were being deeply touched. At the end, after an appeal eight people became Christians and twelve rededicated their lives to the Lord.

We were both awed at what God had done that night, but it was over the next few months that it became clear that He had brought us together for a long-term purpose.

Before this, I had already experienced God speaking to me through His Word and His creation and the everyday things around me. He had revealed His love and compassion to me and as I learnt to listen to Him, the fears and insecurity which had gripped me for so long had begun to melt away.

After I joined Marilyn and started to seek what God wanted to say for the different concerts and to people in need, I was excited to discover that He was revealing new things to me. I started to get pictures, visions, words of knowledge and encouragement which people often responded to, sometimes realising for the first time just how much God loved them. But what really amazed me was the fact that these words came to me in a similar way as when I was hearing Him for myself. As time went by I began to feel a deep longing to help others know that same joy and excitement that I was finding in listening to God my Father.

In 1993 we took part in a conference with writer, Jennifer Rees Larcombe. On the spur of the moment I volunteered to take a workshop on 'creative listening to God' and many of the people who came heard God speaking to them personally for the first time. There was an overwhelming sense of joy and awe as they described what God had shown them. Jennifer came to the workshop and it was at her suggestion that I began to write down some of the principles I had been teaching.

The result is this book!

God wants to talk with you too. As you read through this book you will not find cut and dried methods and techniques of hearing God. I am not writing as an expert, but as someone who has started out on an exciting journey and has still got a long way to go. This journey is not just a means to reaching God at the end, but is in itself the source of joy, excitement and fulfilment because God is walking the whole way with us.

Just as you grow to understand and love a person more as you talk with them and spend time with them, it is my prayer that as you read this book, you will come to understand and love your Heavenly Father more. That you become excited as you realise the scope and depth of the things God wants to share with you. That you are inspired to experiment in the ways you listen to Him.

May it be the start of a lifelong adventure.

Tracy Williamson

PART 1
Laying the Foundations

1
Knowing God as Father

'I love you and want to be a Father to you.'

The wind was blowing harder and the rain was coming down in torrents but I hardly noticed as I sat amazed. God had spoken to me, spoken in such a clear way that I could have no doubt but that this was Him.

'I want to be a Father to you.' The thought kept coming but not as I had thought, an audible voice. It was in my heart that it was speaking and even as I listened it brought with it a deep inner warmth and peace that were totally contrary to the weather and my mood.

I sat on the wooden bench of the old bus shelter and, oblivious to the darkness all around, the trees swaying and groaning in the wind and my complete isolation in this lonely country road, I began to talk with God.

This was my first experience of hearing God and it was the turning point of my Christian life. I had been a Christian for five months and had been going regularly to church, reading my Bible, singing, praying, just like all the other Christians. Yet somehow, something seemed to be missing. As time went by I began to feel a deep despair growing within me. Were God and Christianity going to turn out to be like everything else I had tried? Good in themselves but with no real power in my life? I so longed to be a different person!

That day, a chance remark from another student brought all

the old feelings boiling to the surface. Angry at being deceived in God I decided to leave college. I did not bother to pack but walked off there and then.

Fuelled as I was by anger, I covered many miles in a few hours. Finally the torrential rain forced me to stop when I came to a bus shelter where I sat shivering and remembering the things that had brought me to this place in my life.

I first experienced fear as a very young child. At the age of two and a half I caught measles. A week later my Mum came to get me up but my legs wouldn't support me. Soon I was being rushed off to hospital for tests where doctors told her that my high fever had caused encephalitis, an inflammation of the brain.

After the tests I was left in a ward. Suddenly I seemed to be alone

Alone again now in this dark road, I huddled deeper into my jacket as the fleeting memories came back to me: lying in a cot unable to control my movements, strange faces looking down at me, strange noises. Where was my familiar bed, my room and my toys? Night times were especially frightening without Mummy and Daddy.

Other memories flickered across my mind. Me at school, falling over as I tried to control my wobbly legs, me wearing glasses and surrounded by laughing children calling out 'four eyes'. The exasperated voices of the teachers as I struggled to make sense of words that just sounded a muddle. And all the time, that sick fear that people would notice me and mock me, that somehow I wouldn't match up.

Gazing unseeingly into the night, I couldn't stop the memories coming. I saw myself at seven going downstairs one morning and Mum taking me onto her knee.

'Listen, Tracy,' she said, 'Daddy's gone to heaven.'

I didn't quite hear her, 'Gone to hospital?' I said.

'No, not hospital darling, heaven.'

'Heaven?'

She nodded and her eyes grew more tearful as she gave me a cuddle. Her voice was all funny and choked as she said into my hair, 'Yes, he went in the middle of the night.'

Heaven. What was heaven? I had never heard the term before. Was it another hospital? I didn't know. Mummy was crying and frightened. I ran to my Nan. She too had the tears running down her face and I began to cry myself.

I was confused. I was frightened. Where had Daddy gone?

I remembered that confusion lasting a long time. It was about a year later that the truth finally came home to me that Daddy had gone for good and that I'd never see him again. That night, when everyone was watching the television, I went into the dining room and hid behind the floor length curtains where I wept bitterly.

As other painful memories came flooding into my mind, I rose from the bench and paced around but it was still raining too hard to continue walking. I sat down again and shutting the door on my childhood, saw myself just the year before, arriving at college to take a teaching degree. Full of confidence and hope, I felt that by going to a new place I could throw off my fearful, introverted self and become a new person.

The reality was very different.

I joined many clubs and made some good friends. I liked the course although it was a struggle to follow the lectures. My friends let me photocopy their notes and by doing a lot of background reading, I managed to get fairly good grades in my assignments. But despite all these 'good' things the old fears and insecurities were still ruling me and it was when I did my first major teaching practice that they really took hold.

It was dreadful. All my fears of communicating came to the surface and I felt paralysed as I tried to organise, answer questions and teach new concepts to the children when I couldn't hear them.

By the end of the second week I knew that I couldn't be a teacher.

It was eventually arranged that I would transfer into the BA Degree. In some ways it was a relief when the decision was finally reached but as my dreams of becoming a teacher of the deaf crumbled, my fears and depression reached a new height. I felt confirmed as a failure and despised myself. Everyone thought I was happy with the decision and I found it impossible to communicate what was really happening inside me. The depression took deep hold. Even though I was with people all day, I felt so alone. It wasn't just my deafness, it was the inner conviction that I was useless, that I had nothing to make people like me, that everything I said would be wrong or out of place.

One day, when things had been particularly difficult I went home to my lodgings, dumped my bag into a corner, then set off to the common.

The light was going when I came to the edge of the stream. I stood looking down into the fast flowing waters for a long time, the swirling pattern mesmerised me until it seemed that I was that water, going round and round in circles, no purpose, no goal to aim for. From somewhere deep within me I began to weep. A sense of hopelessness overwhelmed me and I thought how easy it would be to sink into the water forever. As I moved forward I caught my foot on a branch and fell. For a long time I sat shivering on the very edge of the stream then with a violent movement, I twisted around, scrambled back up the bank and ran home.

A week later Ruth, leader of the college Christian Fellowship, asked me to tea. It was a lovely, spring evening and we sat out in the garden. She chatted quietly and I began to relax in her warm friendliness. I commented on the modern appearance of the Bible she had with her and she opened it and began to read bits out to me. The words were unfamiliar as I had no knowledge of the Bible, but they seemed to have a simplicity that I'd never realised. I said so and she laughed and said,

'Well Christianity is simple, it's just about being loved by God.'

'What do you mean?' I asked and Ruth began to explain. She told me about God's love and His anguish when the wrong in our lives prevented us from knowing Him. She told how God's son Jesus, came, knowing and loving each one of us and how by dying, it somehow meant that we could all know God again. She told how He had the power to forgive us and make us different inside, that His love was strong and real enough to make us whole in every way. She told of how He had shown her His love and how much she loved Him now and as she spoke her voice was soft and warm and I could see that love in her eyes.

She gave me some little pamphlets explaining Christianity and one night, I started to read them. One had a little sketch of Jesus on the cross and told why He had died there. As I gazed at it, I seemed to see for the first time that this was a real man struggling and dying. Not just a remote, historical event, but someone who knew me and loved me enough to die for me. I could hardly believe that He loved me, knowing what a mess I was, but as I continued to read, it pointed out again and again with different verses from the Bible, that His love was for everyone, that we simply had to believe and accept it.

Suddenly I knew that I wanted His love for myself. I didn't know how to pray but hesitantly at first I started to speak to Him. As I thought about Him dying for someone like me, tears came to my eyes and I told Him I was sorry I was such a mess and that I believed in Him. Suddenly I became aware that something was happening. It felt as if a heavy, ugly weight was being lifted right out of me and replaced by a deep freedom and peace. Then the realisation came that I wasn't alone. There was no one in the room, yet I knew that someone was with me. I had an overwhelming sense of being loved and accepted.

'Is that you, God?' I asked, amazed, and even though I couldn't see Him or physically touch Him I knew He was there and He loved me.

Soon after this I went to a Christian meeting with the other students and at the end went to the front. A man talked with me about what it meant to be a Christian and encouraged me to start reading the Bible and getting involved with a church. For the first time, I understood that I had become a Christian that night. I went home with a deep sense of excitement and a certainty that now my life was going to change.

Sitting now in the cold bus shelter, I thought bitterly to myself, 'Well, that conviction certainly didn't get me very far, you're no better than anything else, God, if you're there at all!'

It was then, in the midst of all my angry thoughts that I suddenly heard, or rather, felt that voice saying, 'I love you and want to be a Father to you.' I knew it had to be God because I was completely alone.

Bit by bit the same warmth and sense of being loved that I'd experienced the night I became a Christian came to me again. It was almost as though God were sitting next to me on the bench. As I prayed quietly, I realised that although I had been doing all the 'Christian' things, I had never entered into a real give and take relationship with God as my Father. I was holding Him at a distance. Deep within, I sensed Him promising me that He would never, ever leave me, even if I left Him. He would always love me and He wanted me to learn to love and trust Him and to experience His loving care in every part of my life.

The Father Heart of God

God wants to be a Father to us. He wants to talk with us, to tell us how much He loves us, to guide us, to share in our tears and laughter. I have told my story on listening to God at the beginning of this book because it was as I came to understand that God loved me in this way and wanted an ongoing relationship with me, that I was able to truly start communicating with Him

These words of Father love were not just true for me in that particular situation, but are true for all of us. God is the One who is described in the Bible not only as Almighty, the Creator and the only true God, but as Father. 'A father to the fatherless, a defender of widows, is God in His holy dwelling' (Ps. 68:5).

God our Father has called us into relationship with Him as His children and it is as a Father that He calls us to listen to Him. He does not want us to mindlessly respond to His commands out of duty and guilt, but to have an ongoing relationship with Him of love and respect.

We all have Weaknesses

We live in a society today that is dominated by achievement values. Each person is classed by the hidden agenda of what is good or bad. Those who have experienced failure, or who are mentally or physically weak or less able, are often considered inferior and so, in turn, consider themselves inferior while those who are gifted in many ways, or physically strong or beautiful, are the heroes of society.

When I was at senior school I used to dread the games lessons, especially rounders. For this game, the teacher chose two team captains. These two in turn would pick their team and I remember the butterflies beginning to churn in my stomach as one by one the rest of the class were chosen and went to stand with their respective teams. Each week I longed to achieve something in the game that would prevent me from being picked last the following week, but I stayed firmly in that position.

As far as games was concerned, because of my physical limitations I was despised and made to feel useless. There are still some things that I cannot do but that is true for all of us. We may not have physical disabilities but temperamentally and mentally we are all different. Paul, our sound engineer has a very logical, mathematical mind and can solve problems with computers or accounting with ease. He will turn his hand to anything practical and has just completed building a new kitchen for Marilyn. Ask him to do an extended piece of public speaking, however, and he would be terrified!

Marilyn can sing to an audience of several hundred capturing their attention for hours, but ask her to organise the diary and she panics. In fact, at the beginning of her ministry when she was just starting to get requests for concerts she was asked to do one for 300 people. She agreed and the details were decided. A few days later a friend invited her to an end of term party. Marilyn was sure she was free so she said yes. She had a lovely party, got home late and went straight to bed. Early the next morning the phone rang. When she answered a lady said tersely: 'Are you alright?'

'Yes fine,' said Marilyn, rather taken aback.

'Where were you then?'

'What do you mean?' Marilyn asked, very puzzled by now.

'You were meant to be at our church last night for a concert. It was packed out, we'd even got people come off the streets and we waited two hours for you to turn up . . . !'

'Oh my goodness!' Marilyn exclaimed. 'The concert! I'd completely forgotten! I can't have written it down! I don't know how to say sorry . . .'

So there are always things we are less good at and we all take it for granted that at times we need to turn to people who are more qualified to help us.

One day I put some washing in to spin but suddenly the machine gave a piercing scream, jumped out of its corner and hurtled across the floor! Frantically I pushed the buttons and finally, to my intense relief, the deafening noise stopped.

Something was very obviously wrong and I knew I could not sort it out myself. When I called out the engineer he said it was the first time someone had complained of a screaming washing machine that attacked its owner, but he was still able to mend it!

But we can all Hear Him

When it comes to listening to God, we often feel that it is only those who are qualified, like that engineer, who can expect to hear Him. We think to ourselves, 'I'm not spiritual enough. I'm not a leader, I don't do anything for God. I just go to church.' When we've got problems or need guidance we think that if we talk to someone 'high up' or 'up front' they will be able to hear God for us and provide us with a solution.

My Sheep Hear My Voice

But the criterion for being able to hear God is not how clever or qualified we are, nor our position in the church. What it solely depends on is whether or not we are one of God's children.

Jesus, comparing Himself to a shepherd, said, 'the sheep listen to his voice. He calls his own sheep by name and leads them out' (John 10:3).

Jesus describes us as His sheep. He says He knows us by name and that we listen to Him. As we listen, He leads us. This is an active, direct, personal relationship. Any other way is like a child always relating to his father through his mother. Sadly, many children do have to do this because their fathers are too violent for them to go to directly, but God is a Father who loves us and longs to speak to us and give to us. 'How much more then will your Father in heaven give . . . to those who ask Him' (Luke 11:13).

Many of us Robbed

God wants a tender, affirming relationship with us. But many of us have been robbed of a true understanding of what a father's love is meant to be, by our experience with our own fathers.

I remember one girl called Anne, who came up to Marilyn and me at the end of a concert one morning.

'Hello,' I said, smiling at her, 'did you want to chat with us about something?'

She nodded, her head bowed so that her hair swung over her face, obscuring it. Without speaking she sat down in the chair next to Marilyn and seemed to be struggling to know what to say. I tried to encourage her to open up.

'Did something in the concert touch you?'

She paused, then looked up.

'Yes,' she said, she hesitated again, then her words came quickly, almost tumbling over each other. 'You talked in the concert about God loving us and wanting to be a real father and friend to us, wanting to speak to us and guide us, but I can't believe God wants to be like that with me!' She stared at me for a moment and then dropped her eyes and started fiddling with her handbag strap.

Marilyn leaned forward and took her hand. 'You may not feel God will want to be a friend to you,' she said, 'but that isn't what He says. He says He doesn't have any favourites and loves us all as His children.'

The girl remained silent, staring down at her lap.

'How did your own father treat you?' Marilyn asked quietly.

A sigh ran through her. She looked up at us briefly then turned away and gazed out of the nearby doorway.

'My father?' she said, and the tone of her voice was low and flat so that even Marilyn had to lean forward to hear her. 'I hardly knew I had a father. He never spoke to me or if he did it was only to ridicule me when I tried to speak to him. I tried so hard to please him but I might just as well not have been there.' She buried her face in her hands and her voice became choked with tears. 'I feel there's nothing worth loving in me . . .'

This situation is one that happens all too often. Anne had longed for her father to acknowledge her, to talk to her, to listen to the things she wanted to share with him. But he had constantly ignored or ridiculed her. The effects of this were real and obvious. Unable to believe herself worth loving she in turn, was unable to communicate. This alienated people which, in a vicious circle, confirmed her inner belief that she was unlovable. The more this happened the less she was able to believe in and enjoy God's love. Yet this emotionally crippled young woman knew deep down that she should have been communicated with, that she had been robbed of something that was her true right.

God Lavishes Love

In John's first letter the Father love of God is expressed in a wonderful way, 'How great is the love the Father has lavished on us that we should be called children of God and that is what we are!' (1 John 3:1).

Anne experienced total rejection from her earthly father but her Heavenly Father wanted to 'lavish' love on her. My pocket Oxford Dictionary describes 'lavish' as 'giving or producing something in large quantities'. The quantities of love God wants to pour out on us are limitless and unconditional. He never holds back but responds to us even before we've spoken!

The Communicating Heart of God

Communicating is what enables us to live and blossom as people. Even before babies show any awareness of their surroundings, they respond to their mother's smile. Their first words are copies of hers and in a remarkably short time they are able to express their own thoughts. What God has made such a natural element of our lives is also a natural element of His. From the first pages of the Bible, God is shown to be a communicator. He simply spoke and the unformed chaos of the masses listened and responded and His perfect order and beauty came into being. 'And God said "let there be light" and there was light' (Gen. 1:3).

God desired and planned from the very beginning to be known, loved and responded to, that is why He created man. 'Then God said "Let us make man in our image, in our likeness"' (Gen. 1:26).

And the first thing God did with man was speak to him. He gave Adam clear and specific instructions, showing him what his responsibility was to be as His partner in ruling the world. He did not speak as a being who was remote and abstract, cut off from the practical realities of life, but as one who, even at this earliest stage of creation, understood man's needs and wanted to meet them. As He spoke, He gave Adam self worth and fulfilment by providing a role that would enable him to be stretched mentally. In declaring that 'It is not good for the man to be alone, I will make a helper suitable for him' (Gen. 2:18), He provided for Adam's emotional and physical needs. He gave Adam and his wife a beautiful home and often came Himself to spend time with them there. In every way He showed that He cared and loved them as a father.

Communication Breakdown!

This idyllic relationship between God and man broke down when Adam and Eve, believing the lies of the devil, disowned

God and tried to go their own way. It is revealing that in this first example of the way Satan tempts man, it was the words of God and our ability to correctly hear Him that he threw into doubt. Eve believed him and so began the tragedy of man turning away from God and the whole purpose of his existence.

God, however, never let that purpose die completely. The Bible shows that from generation to generation God continued to call to man, seeking out those who would be open to hearing His voice. Every time an individual responded to the merest whisper, God would make Himself known and would begin to speak openly and deeply of His heart and purposes. Those who responded, believing, loving and obeying His words became His messengers to the rest of the people. For it has always been God's desire and longing not just for individuals to know and hear Him but for everyone to be able to do this. 'I will be their God and they will be my people. No longer will a man teach his neighbour or a man his brother, saying "know the Lord" for they will all know me, from the least of them to the greatest' (Jer. 31:33–4).

How can we know God as Father now?

God wants to be a father to all of us but this does not happen automatically. If that were the case there would have been no reason for Jesus' death on the cross. God knew that there was no way we would be able to reach Him ourselves because from the very beginning we had deliberately turned our backs on Him and so, because He loved us He came Himself, as Jesus.

Jesus did not just set us a good example or show us what God was like. He did an even more radical thing – He died for us. Somehow, in an incredible way, as He suffered that agonising death and separation from His Father, God, he broke down for ever the wall of separation between *us* and God, 'but now, in Christ Jesus you who were once far away have been brought near through the blood of Christ. For He Himself is our peace who has made the two one and has destroyed the barrier, the dividing wall of hostility' (Eph. 2:13–14).

For years I vaguely thought there might be a God out there somewhere. I knew the Lord's Prayer and had sung hymns at junior school about Jesus dying for our sins. But it wasn't until I prayed that night in my room and told Jesus that I believed He had died for *me* and I wanted His forgiveness and love for myself, that God became real to me. I became a Christian because I *believed* what Jesus had done for me.

John 3:16 says: 'For God so loved the world [that's me and you!] that He gave His one and only Son *that whoever believes in Him* [my italics] shall not perish but have eternal life.'

Believing is the criterion for becoming a child of God and therefore having the right to hear Him and talk with Him. That is why it is nothing to do with how clever or able we are. All God wants us to do is believe – He's done all the rest!

Maybe at this point you've realised deep down in your heart that you've never really believed in Jesus. You've never asked Him to forgive you and show you His love. Maybe you've realised that although you've always known about God, you don't know Him as your own Heavenly Father.

You can know God in that way right now. Right where you are you can talk to Him and He will hear you and answer you. You could pray something like this:

Thank you that you love me so much. Thank you Lord Jesus that you died for me. Please forgive me, I want to know your love and to be with you from now on. Thank you that you have made me your child and you are my Heavenly Father. Please help me to know you and to love you. Amen.

If you have prayed this for the first time you have become a Christian. You now have the right to come close to your Father

God and start to talk to Him about anything and everything. He wants to talk with you, to comfort you, to guide you, to share His thoughts about this world with you. It's the start of an exciting journey and as you continue to read through this book you will start learning the many and exciting ways through which your Father God wants to talk to you.

2
Be Filled With the Holy Spirit

In 1 Corinthians there is a passage which is exciting and far reaching in its implications. 'No eye has seen, no ear has heard, no mind has conceived what God has prepared for those who love Him . . . But God has revealed it to us by His Spirit' (1 Cor. 2:9–10).

We cannot even begin to know God's thoughts and purposes, let alone dare to say that we can hear Him, yet Paul is saying that God has given us His very own Spirit. 'We have not received the spirit of the world but the Spirit who is from God, that we may understand what God has freely given us' (1 Cor. 2:12).

This is the same Spirit who was behind the creation of this beautiful world, who inspired and anointed men to speak God's truth in the Old Testament and who came upon Jesus Christ in divine power from the time of His baptism. The passage ends with more amazing words, 'For who has known the mind of the Lord, that he may instruct him? But we have the mind of Christ' (1 Cor. 2:16).

What man cannot do, God has done for man. By renewing our minds and giving us His Holy Spirit, He has opened the door for us to have the awesome privilege of drawing close and listening to Him.

Something Missing

When I first became a Christian I knew without any doubt that Jesus had come close to me and forgiven me. After that experience at the bus stop, I started to relate to Him as my Father as well as my Saviour, but there was still something missing. When I went to church I often looked around at people's faces as they worshipped and was moved by their expressive love for God. Many were raising their hands, almost as if they were embracing Him, some were smiling deep tender smiles, some were even crying. I was deeply touched and longed to be able to worship and love Jesus like this myself but when I tried I couldn't. I sang the choruses along with everyone else but I felt full of fear and inhibition and I knew there was a real hollowness in my expressions of love to Him. I thought it must just be that these people were more extrovert than I, but when I got to know them more I realised that wasn't necessarily true. Some were, of course, but others seemed as shy as me and yet they were still able to express love to God.

Hearing God's Words and Strategies

Frequently, in the service people would tell how God had led them to go and speak to a certain person, or given them just what they needed to say in a certain situation, often with dramatic results. Or they would speak out messages from His heart as if He Himself was speaking to us. Someone had such a message for me shortly after I became a Christian. I realised that it expressed God's desire to speak to me in this same intimate way and was amazed. I longed to be able to hear God like this and every day I would try with all my might, but all I ever heard were my own thoughts buzzing around!

The Holy Spirit

When I asked my friends how they could talk so freely about Jesus and how they could hear His thoughts and know His strategies, they kept saying that it was the Holy Spirit. Diana explained, seeing that I still looked puzzled, that as the third person of God, the Holy Spirit wanted to fill our lives with the life and power of Jesus. She showed me the verses describing how Jesus Himself was filled with the Holy Spirit after He was baptised and how from that time on He was led and empowered to do miracles, speak words of authority and be guided in every step right through to His death. She explained it was God's plan that as Jesus died and was resurrected the same Holy Spirit would be given to each person who believed in Jesus so that ordinary men and women could become like Him.

The Disciples Were Weak . . .

I had sometimes thought how much easier it must have been for the early disciples because they had actually been with Jesus, but as I read the Bible I was interested to see how human they were. They were full of grief and fear as it suddenly came home to them that they were going to lose Him. After all the miracles and incredible demonstrations of God's power and those intimate times when He would talk deeply and personally with them over dinner. After becoming more and more aware that this was no ordinary man but was actually the Son of God, now He was going to leave them. Had everything been in vain? How could they possibly carry on if Jesus were not with them?

Into all this turmoil, Jesus spoke these amazing words, 'Because I have said these things you are filled with grief. But I tell you the truth, it is for your good that I am going away. Unless I go away the Counsellor will not come to you, but if I go I will send Him to you' (John 16:7).

Jesus kept on talking about the Counsellor who was to come, saying that He would remind them of what Jesus had said and give them the power to know His thoughts and speak His words. That He wouldn't just be with them but would actually be inside them. That through the Holy Spirit the very life and presence of Jesus would be with all of them always.

The Promise Fulfilled

Diana continued to explain to me how once Jesus had risen this promise was fulfilled and the disciples were filled in a definite way with the Holy Spirit. As we looked at the different verses, I was amazed and excited as I saw how their lives were transformed after this. They had been so weak and fearful before, all running away as soon as the going got tough and now they were standing in front of a hostile crowd talking eloquently and powerfully about Jesus, so powerfully that huge numbers became Christians in one day.

'You see,' Diana said, 'Jesus promised that the Holy Spirit would remind them of everything Jesus had said and that is what is happening here. And look,' she flicked over the pages and pointed her finger at the story of Ananias and Sapphira (Acts 5:1–10). 'Here's an example of Peter suddenly knowing something that he couldn't have known humanly. That's what Jesus did all the time and now they are too. That same thing was happening on Sunday when David was sharing those thoughts about different people. The Bible calls it "the word, or message of knowledge" in 1 Corinthians 12:8, and we can receive that ability when the Holy Spirit fills us.'

'But how does the Holy Spirit fill us?'

'You ask Him!' said Diana simply. She turned the pages back to the Gospels. 'Look at what Jesus said.' She passed it to me and I read:

> Which of you fathers, if your son asks for a fish, will give him a snake instead? Or if he asks for an egg, will give him a scorpion? If you then, though you are evil, know how to give good gifts to your children, how much more will your Father in heaven give the Holy Spirit to those who ask Him! (Luke 11:11–13)

I was deeply stirred by this conversation. I had experienced enough of God's love already to make me long for more and I was excited at the prospect of being able to hear God guiding me, giving me power to love Him and tell people about Him. As I continued to read through the Bible I realised for the first time how the Holy Spirit had been at work from the very beginning, first in the act of creation, then again and again inspiring and empowering individuals to do God's will, until the time came when He was given to every believer.

Soon after this I went forward at the end of a Christian meeting and a man laid hands on me and prayed for me to receive the Holy Spirit. Unlike the night I became a Christian this was not an emotional experience and I wondered if anything had happened. The man told me not to go by feelings which were often unreliable, but to simply thank God that what I had asked for, He had heard and answered.

New Vision and Understanding

My first realisation that God had answered my prayer came the next morning. As I walked up the college drive, I suddenly became aware of the beauty of the surrounding countryside. I stopped and looked around, taking a deep breath. Everything seemed to be painted in a fresh new colour. I gazed at the brightness of the green fields stretching into the distance, broken only by the magnificent plane trees; at the softness of the early morning blue sky and the brightness of the tiny wild flowers peeping through the reeds. It was as if I had never seen them before, yet I walked up this same drive three or four times every day. As I stood still I understood afresh that this was all God's handiwork. It was as if He was standing next to me whispering, 'I did all this for you and now I am teaching you how to really see it.' I suddenly remembered the verse in Corinthians where it says, 'God has revealed it to us by His Spirit' (1 Cor. 3:10).

My first lecture was in 'Education'. That morning we were discussing the concept of freedom in relation to education and suddenly the tutor turned to me.

'What do you think about this, Tracy?' she asked.

Aware of everyone's eyes on me I sent up an urgent prayer. Suddenly an idea came to my mind. I was startled by it but couldn't think of anything else so blurted it out.

'The Bible says that if the "Son of Man sets us free we will be free indeed".'

Mrs Pearson peered at me over the top of her glasses.

'We are discussing freedom in education, not religion, Tracy.'

'Yes, but if we know the true inner freedom that comes from knowing God, then that would affect everything including our decisions in education.' I paused, amazed both at my daring and at the thought.

Mrs Pearson said 'Humph' and shook her head. She was about to call on somebody else when Steven suddenly spoke up.

'You know, I think Tracy's right,' he said. 'We always try to compartmentalise things so much. I'm not sure what I think about the religious side of it but I think it's true that we should find out what freedom really means at its grass roots before we can clarify what it means in relation to specialist areas.'

John chimed in, 'Yes I agree. I think we should be considering the . . .'

His voice was lost to me as several of them began to speak at once. I sat dazed. I had never before said anything to spark off a discussion like this, but it wasn't just that, it was the thought itself. I knew that my mind had been blank when Mrs Pearson spoke to me and yet suddenly this idea had gripped me with a real certainty of its rightness. Suddenly I remembered that it was as I had sent up that S.O.S. prayer that the thought had come.

'Lord,' I prayed, as the others continued to talk excitedly. 'Was that you giving me this thought?'

I sensed Him answering 'Yes!' I did not say anything more in that seminar but continued to pray quietly. A deep sense of awe began to fill me and I knew that God had indeed answered my prayer last night. Not with a 'big bang' emotional experience but by coming alongside me just like a close friend, opening my eyes afresh to beauty and my ears to things I'd never thought of before.

Over the next few weeks and months I learnt more of what it could mean to be filled with the Holy Spirit of God. I began to discover that God did not just want to counsel me in 'churchy' situations but at all times, just like that first time in my lecture. Bit by bit I learnt to recognise His voice, to hear the things that He wanted me to do and to depend on His power as I did them, to know the things that made Him happy or sad, to receive the gifts that He wanted to give me. The more I experienced Him filling me, speaking to me, the more my fears of openly being a Christian began to melt away.

What Does it Mean to be Full?

Maybe the idea of being full of God seems too abstract to be real when you're faced with the day's mountain of problems. But in our day-to-day lives we can become full of things that completely alter our outlook. Take my friend Judith for example. I arrived home one day and was looking forward to a nice chat.

'You look happy!' I remarked casually as we sat down with our drinks.

'I am,' she said, 'really happy!'

I laughed at her excited look. 'What's happened then?'

'Well, you know when I talked to you about Cefyn?' She glanced at me sideways and I smiled at the tell-tale blush. 'Well, the thing is, we went out in a sort of trial way and,' she paused and then spoke in a rush, 'I really like him.'

'Oh that's fantastic,' I said, 'So are you going out properly now then?'

She nodded. 'Yes, since last week.' She took a few sips of coffee and then said musingly, 'You know, it's funny, when he first suggested going out I thought we were too different and I couldn't see that we would have anything much to say to each other. But we had loads, and he seems to know exactly the sort of things I like. He gave me these cards, for example, saying that when he saw them he felt they were really me and they are, I love the design of them!'

Her eyes sparkling she continued telling me about Cefyn, his kindness and the way he always seemed to know what she was thinking. His love of fun combined with his sensitivity . . . she was full of him and I was thrilled for her. As I listened, I marvelled anew at the power of love to transform us. Just a few weeks before Judith had been tired and over-burdened with her work load, now although that was still the same, her new found love for Cefyn seemed to have lifted the strain and given her a radiant lease of life.

The difference for my friend, as for all of us when we meet someone we love, was that she moved from the place where she knew Cefyn as an acquaintance, to beginning to know him in a much more intimate way. Already at this early stage, her thoughts and feelings were full of him.

The Intimacy of Love

The incredible thing is, that what we experience and take for granted as normal in our human relationships, is also true for our relationship with God. God wants us to be full of Him. Not just knowing Him at a distance, but intimately, so that our very thoughts and feelings are focused on His thoughts and feelings. So that we are taken up with the things that He loves, and able to receive the things that He wants to give us. He said He did not just want us to be following rules and regulations out of duty but for His ways and desires to be actually engraved on our hearts. '"This is the covenant that I will make with the house of Israel after that time," declares the Lord. "I will put my law in their minds and write it on their hearts. I will be their God and they will be my people"' (Jer. 31:33).

God's ways are engraved on our hearts, not by us trying as hard as we can, but simply by us being filled with the Holy Spirit.

Recently I was travelling on a train and tried to lift my heavy suitcase onto the overhead rack. Being taller than the average woman, I thought it would be an easy task. I managed to get the edge of the case onto the edge of the rack but that was as far as I got. I pushed, I shoved, I tried wriggling it bit by bit. My arms were shaking like leaves and sweat was dripping off me. Finally I tried jumping up and pushing at the same time. The case went back a couple of inches but as I landed I lost my balance and my grip on the edge of the case. It crashed through my arms, hit the table, turned over and thudded into an elderly man's lap. A stunned silence filled the carriage!

Red with embarrassment and apologising profusely I braced myself for a second attempt. As I lifted it a middle-aged man offered me his help. He picked up the case, lifted it up and in two seconds had it securely on the shelf!

The point is, we may be very nice people, we may have lots of abilities and a strong moral sense. We may have a desire to serve God and to hear His voice, but just as I needed that man to lift my case for me, so we need the power of the Holy Spirit to fill us, transform our thoughts and feelings, and enable us to be effective for God.

My First Picture

Some time after I asked Jesus to fill me with the Holy Spirit, I was in my church one Sunday. Worship songs were playing and people were beginning to open up to God and express their love to Him. I was still having problems in letting go in worship and I started to get the usual feelings of inhibition and fear. In desperation I prayed, 'Lord you know how much I long to express love to you. Please show me yourself in such a way that I can give myself in love to you without fear.'

Suddenly as I stood with my eyes closed, I saw the face of Jesus smiling at me. I gazed at Him in wonder. He seemed to be holding His arms out to me and without thinking I lifted my hands and put them into His. I stood there drinking in His love until the vision faded. When I opened my eyes I was amazed to find that I was standing in the same attitude of worship as those I'd been envying for their freedom for so long. The Holy Spirit had answered my prayer and I remembered the verses in Joel where it says that when the Spirit comes people will dream dreams and see visions. He had given me a vision to make me fall in love with Jesus.

To Hear, we Need the Holy Spirit

Throughout this book we will be looking at the many ways of hearing God, but we cannot try, or enjoy, any of them without the Holy Spirit's enabling. He is the one who will open our ears and teach us the deep things of God. He is the one who will make the Word of God alive and real to us. He is the one who will give us the power to tell people about Jesus and will fill our hearts with love for Him.

Have you been filled with the Holy Spirit of God? Not just in a one-off experience, but every day, today? Paul said 'be filled with the Holy Spirit'. That means all the time.

Your Heavenly Father will give you the Holy Spirit if you ask Him. You could ask right now, and as simply as Him forgiving you, He will fill you. You could pray something like this:

> **Father God, thank you that you promised me the Holy Spirit to be my Counsellor, to teach me about Jesus, and to enable me to do the things that Jesus did. Lord, I ask that you will**

give me what you have promised. Please fill me, Holy Spirit. Let me hear your voice and receive all the things you want to give me. Thank you that you have heard this prayer and are answering it. In Jesus' name. Amen.

PART 2

Ways of Hearing God

3
Listening Through His Word

'I have hidden your word in my heart' (Psalm 119:11)

I once read a book by a poor Korean pastor. He had none of the basic amenities that most of us take for granted and everything he owned was precious to him. While describing his life, he made a passing comment that really caught my attention and has stayed in my mind, despite the fact that it is now about ten years since I read it. This is what it was: 'When I pick up the most precious material possession I own, my Bible . . .'[1]

I could tell, as I read further, that this man truly loved the Bible. To him it was not just a book but the living, loving Word of his Heavenly Father. As he sat on his one chair in his dark little room, he devoured the Bible day and night, seeking to know his Father more and more deeply, meditating, studying, drinking in the truths until his life was saturated with them and still he continued. The effects of this prayerful love of God through His Word were dramatic and far reaching, for this poor, unknown man, Paul Yonggi Cho, became in a comparatively short time, the leader of what is claimed to be the world's biggest and fastest growing Church.

The Bible was Cho's most precious possession. As I thought about what this really mean, these words struck deep into my heart. I knew that I did not have anywhere near the same devotion for the Bible. It was something that needed to be read now that I was a Christian. I knew that it was God's living

Word and therefore holy and of sacred importance, but this man was talking in such a personal intimate way of his love for the Bible.

Sitting on the settee I read the phrase again, then laid the book down with a sigh. If the Bible isn't so precious to me then what is, I thought. As I gazed around the room I realised that it was things like my photographs and my personal papers that were coming to mind. Things that would most give me a vivid remembrance of someone I had loved, and a sense of personal belonging and identity.

Glancing at my Bible again, I suddenly understood that it is these very same qualities that make it God's living, precious Word to us. It is through the Bible that we develop a heart picture of God and what He is like. We begin to perceive His greatness and awesome power and to understand His heart, how He thinks and feels and what He is doing. This is equivalent to my photographs. Secondly, it is through the Bible that we learn that we are God's dearly loved children, heirs together with Jesus, His servants, His priests, His friends, His arms and legs . . . That is our identity, equivalent to my papers. We cling onto our birth certificates because they are proof of who we are and all of us need that confirmation that our names were chosen for us and that we fit into the scheme of things. But where the certificate is just a scrap of paper containing the barest details, the Bible gives us an incredibly awesome picture of who we are in God's eyes and how we fit into *His* scheme of things.

The more I thought about this the more aware I became of what Yonggi Cho was feeling when he talked about the Bible being the most precious of his possessions. A deep sense of excitement and longing began to fill me as I glimpsed the truth that through His Word, I could come to know God more and more deeply. I knew that I could not, as yet, make the same claim as Cho, but right then I prayed and asked God to change me and give me a heart that loved Him and ears to hear Him through His Word.

Preconceived Ideas

One night, when I was a child, I couldn't sleep so I went to the bookshelf looking for something exciting. Suddenly, my eye was drawn to the little Bible tucked in at the end. I pulled it out, flicked back the cover and glanced through the pages. I didn't know where to start so just dipped in at random. The writing was tiny and very difficult to read but I persevered in trying to make sense of it. After half an hour I had to give up. My eyes were heavy with tiredness and I could hardly understand the words let alone take in what it was saying. I felt a deep sense of disappointment as I closed the Bible and placed it back on the shelf. It had simply confirmed that God, if He existed at all, was unreachable and irrelevant.

Nine years later, when I first became a Christian that experience was buried deep in my subconscious. I believed that the Bible would be boring and impossible to understand. I was already beginning to love reading Christian books but when my friends pointed out the need for me to read the Bible every day, I felt a distinct lack of desire.

One evening I went for tea with my friends John and Amanda and found myself expressing some of the sadnesses and fears that so often bound me. Amanda listened quietly and then got up and went outside. When she returned she had a Bible in her hands and my heart began to sink. Now, I thought, we're going to get into all this heavy incomprehensible stuff.

Sitting next to me she opened the Bible, flicked through the pages and then handed it to me.

'Read that,' she said, 'and especially take note of the ending verses.'

Rather uncertainly I began to read, 'he who created you, O

Jacob, he who formed you, O Israel: "Fear not, for I have redeemed you; I have summoned you by name; you are mine . . . Since you are precious and honoured in my sight, and because I love you"' (Isa. 43:1–4).

At first, I did not understand. God was talking to Israel and Jacob so why was Amanda so insistent I read it? But when I asked her, she said that although God had originally spoken to Israel and Jacob, it was actually addressed to all His people, all Christians and therefore to me too.

'When you read the Bible, Tracy,' she said, 'you've got to read it with the attitude that God is also speaking to you personally through these words. So for example,' she pointed to the last verses, 'when God says you are precious and honoured in His sight, that means you personally, Tracy.' She stopped and looked at me in the eyes.

'His Word is the truth about you. That's why it's so important you read it and drink it in. It's as if it is a book full of His letters to you. In His letters He tells you what He is like and what He feels about you, but you must realise that even though it was written so long ago, He had you in mind when He wrote it. Look at this.'

She flicked through to another page and pointed at the verse. 'For He chose us in Him before the creation of the world to be holy and blameless in His sight' (Eph. 1:4).

'You see,' she said, smiling at me, 'this was written a very long time after the creation of the world, yet it says that God knew you and planned for you to belong to Him before anything else was made.'

I took the Bible and read the verses slowly, still not sure what Amanda was getting at.

'Imagine He is sitting here with you on the settee and telling you these things.'

I looked up at her as she said this and something about the kindness in her eyes touched me deep inside. I suddenly knew that Jesus was there, loving me, and that He really did want to speak to me through these verses. I read them again, trying to imagine that Jesus was saying these very words to me, that I was precious and honoured, and that I had been thought about and created for a wonderful purpose.

As I reflected, I suddenly remembered a time when I was about eleven. It was coming up to Easter and our teacher asked us all to make Easter hats and decorate them for a special Easter assembly. There would be a prize for the prettiest hat.

When Mrs Ashton called us all to come and display our hats mine still looked like a flat pancake. It didn't even have a rim yet and surely the head part was meant to be bigger and deeper or it wouldn't stay on? When it was my turn I rammed it firmly on my head and walked forward as steadily as I could. I managed about three steps and then it slid off and fluttered to the floor.

The other children started to titter as Mrs Ashton picked it up and turned it over.

'You don't seem to be managing very well, Tracy.'

I looked down blushing with shame while she quickly scanned the rest of the class.

'Julie, you've worked very quickly on your hat, you can make Tracy one too.'

She screwed mine up, dropped it into the bin and turned to the next child while I shuffled back to my seat wishing the floor would swallow me up.

As I remembered this incident and felt again that sense of shame and failure, I suddenly 'heard' the Lord speaking these words to me:

'You created that hat in love because you knew in your heart how you wanted it to look. You chose the colours and you were excited as you imagined the finished result. When your teacher discarded it and crushed it in her hand to throw away you felt sad, because even though it hadn't come out right it was still your creation. My child, I too have created you in love and I too chose the different colours that would make you unique as a person. From the very beginning of time I have felt excitement and joy about you because I knew what I was going to do with your life. I too have grieved when the different circumstances of your life have crushed you and made you feel a mistake. But my child, unlike your teacher, I will not discard you. You often discard yourself but my purposes for you still stand the same. Just as your hat was precious to you so you are precious to me but where your hat was mocked and rejected, I tell you that you are loved and honoured and my perfect purposes for you will be fulfilled.'

I sat amazed as I received these words from God. I knew that I could not have made them up, my feelings said so much the opposite. I had totally forgotten that childish incident, but God knew the memory needed transforming by His words of truth. Before, I had just skimmed over that passage thinking that such lovely words could never apply to me. The moment I started to read them with my heart and asked God to make them real to me, they came to life in a deeply personal way.

This experience taught me that my preconceived assumptions that the Bible was dull and irrelevant were wrong. I had been deceived by the outward things of that night-time experience and the fact that at numerous times throughout my education the Bible was dismissed as 'just good literature', 'a form of escapism for those who can't face reality' and even 'pure rubbish'.

Maybe you think these things don't matter, after all when we become Christians we learn that the Bible is the living Word of God and our attitudes are changed, so what difference does it make what we've heard before?

I believe they do matter, to the degree that if we are not aware of their existence it is possible to go through our entire Christian lives with a negative attitude to the Bible buried deep in our subconscious. Remember, we have an enemy who hates us to believe and love God's Word. He will do anything he can to make us avoid reading it and if there have been any negative seeds sown he will make sure that those previous judgments and feelings will still be influencing us even if we do read it .

Romans 12:2 says, 'Do not conform any longer to the pattern of this world, but be transformed by the renewing of your mind. Then you will be able to test and approve what God's will is—His good, pleasing and perfect will.'

This implies that change is not just an automatic result of becoming a Christian but that it is as we consciously stand against those things where we have just been following the trend, and start taking hold of the truth instead, that true transformation will come. In my case, it was as I started reading books like Yonggi Cho's and spent time with friends who loved the Bible, that I realised my attitude towards it was wrong. When God spoke to me that evening my heart changed as I began to understand the way that God wanted to speak to me through His Word.

A Prayer

Lord God, you say that your Word is living and active and that it is meant to be a joy and delight to me. But Lord I often feel that to read it is the least thing I want to do, there are so many other things that seem more exciting. Lord I ask that you will reveal to me any past attitudes or judgments about the Bible that I took on board and that are still influencing me now. Please forgive me Lord and help me to stand against them. In Jesus' name. Amen.

The Holy Spirit as Counsellor

Following his comment about the Bible being his most precious possession, Cho continues: 'I pray to the Holy Spirit, "O Holy

Spirit, open my eyes so I may see the Truth of God in Thy Holy Word." What a joy it is to study the Word of God after prayer.'[2]

Jesus said that He was sending us the Holy Spirit to be our counsellor and to teach us everything He had told us. We are absolutely dependent on Him because the Bible is not just theories and rules which, if we follow carefully, will bring about certain results for us. Rather, it is spiritually imparted truths that have a dynamic life and power inherent within them that no ordinary book could ever have. 'For the word of God is living and active. Sharper than any double-edged sword, it penetrates even to dividing soul and spirit, joints and marrow; it judges the thoughts and attitudes of the heart' (Heb. 4:12).

It is possible to read it on a completely superficial level. To understand the general essence of what it is saying but to miss the depth of spiritual insight and knowledge that lies behind it. In order to discern what it is really saying and the heart of the Person saying it, we need like Cho, to ask the Holy Spirit to come and be our counsellor and teacher.

When I was first a Christian I felt very frustrated. People in my church used to talk about how powerful and anointed the teaching was but I couldn't hear it! One day I was moaning about this to a friend and she made a comment that transformed my way of thinking.

'You know, Trace, you don't have to be dependent on other people's teaching,' she said. 'God can teach you Himself through His Word by His Holy Spirit. After all, the first apostles didn't have a handy New Testament to go by. It's true they had been with Jesus but the things they taught in the letters were in much fuller detail than Jesus' teachings, and besides, if you think of Paul, he hadn't been with Jesus at all and even after he became a Christian he didn't spend any time at first with the others but just went straight out and started teaching. Yet he received so much revelation from God that his teaching forms the major part of the New Testament.'

I stared at her. 'So can I just ask God to come and teach me then, but how does He do it?'

My friend gave me some ideas and over the next few weeks I began to try them out. Like Cho, I started to pray to the Holy Spirit to come and make the passage I was reading each day alive to me. Rather than just picking out any odd verse at random to suit my mood, I tried to follow a set plan of reading through the whole Bible, but keeping alert to any particular verse or passage that seemed to become significant. I tried to consciously imagine Him sitting next to me as I read, and pointing out different things to me, which I would then 'discuss' in prayer with Him.

It reminded me of when I started at primary school and was learning to read. I remember struggling over the new spellings and my dad patiently sitting with me and helping me to 'see' each word with new eyes. Then came the day when suddenly the words stopped looking like a mad jumble on the page and suddenly made sense. From that moment a passion for reading was born that has never died since.

I began to find that as I read and prayed in this way new ideas and interpretations were illuminated in my mind. It was as if the Holy Spirit was highlighting a word or a verse and saying, 'Look this means that' or 'Can you see what that is revealing about God's heart?' 'Can you see how this is being fulfilled in the world now?' Sometimes a passage would completely puzzle me and I would ask Him what it meant and gradually learnt that if I kept mulling it over in my mind throughout the day, insights would develop later. Since then, bit by bit over the months and years my understanding has grown and the more I receive the more I want to know.

I have now been a Christian for thirteen years and for ten of those years I have worked with Marilyn. From the very beginning Marilyn asked me if I could share thoughts from the Bible in the concerts and occasionally these have developed into quite major teaching spots, yet I have never heard a sermon for myself! This is not just a special grace to me to make up for not hearing, but something that God longs for us all to be experiencing as well as being taught and challenged by the anointed teachers we all flock to hear.

The Power of God's Word . . .

At the beginning of this chapter I described how as I read a Bible passage my old negative concepts about myself began to change. This was because the Word of God is true. Because it is true it contains an incredible power.

This is what the Bible says about itself:

> And the words of the Lord are flawless, like silver refined in a furnace of clay, purified seven times.(Ps. 12:6)
>
> The law of the Lord is perfect, reviving the soul. The statutes of the Lord are trustworthy, making wise the simple. The precepts of the Lord are right, giving joy to the heart. The commands of the Lord are radiant, giving light to the eyes. (Ps. 19:7–8)
>
> I, the Lord, speak the truth; I declare what is right. (Isa. 45:19)
>
> 'Is not my word like fire,' declares the Lord, 'and like a hammer that breaks a rock in pieces?' (Jer. 23:29)
>
> Man does not live on bread alone, but on every word that comes from the mouth of God. (Deut. 8:3, Matt. 4:4)
>
> Faith comes from hearing . . . the word of Christ. (Rom. 10:17)
>
> Take the . . . sword of the Spirit, which is the word of God. (Eph. 6:17)

Again and again God emphasises the importance of drinking in the truth of His Word, feeding on it, using it as a weapon, standing on it, believing it, living it.

. . . To Destroy the Negative Words that Destroy us

In the West our culture and society is dominated by words. They scream at us night and day, from papers and posters; from unwanted mail telling us that unless we have a certain life insurance our families will suffer, unless we give to this charity other people will suffer. Words call seductively from the TV and radio that we must be slim, must have this outfit, new home, sexual experience etc. Words come at us from our parents from the moment we are born and later from friends, teachers, colleagues, partners, children . . .

Often these words will be full of love and affirmation encouraging us to go on in life, to grow in confidence and self worth. Words of this nature are wonderful and vitally important, but sadly the words that many people experience are full of rejection, scorn and mockery.

Instead of building us up these words bind us and destroy our confidence. Instead of blossoming into adulthood we wilt and hide ourselves or we live in an impossible race to earn the approval we so long for. I think of my friend whose parents were disappointed that she was not a boy and constantly mocked her developing femininity, or a lady we met whose father told her repeatedly as a little girl that her schoolwork was never good enough and she would always be a failure. In her book *Turning Point*, Jennifer Rees Larcombe describes how she was put into a bondage of fear and striving by a teacher who described her as the 'stupidest child she had ever had the misfortune to teach,'[3] and through her father's words Marilyn has lived most of her life in fear of being a nuisance.

Most of us think we can just shrug these things off and don't realise that when we feel that fear gripping us inside as we face a particular situation, or go to the doctor's to get more tranquillisers, we are living out these negative words. They have become like chains binding us and no self persuasion or good intentions can break those chains. But Jesus Christ can and will break them as we trust in Him and in *His* Word.

We need to ask God to take us to a verse or passage that can act as an antidote to the negative words we've received. Then we can ask the Holy Spirit to make the words real to us and reveal all its hidden meaning. We need to give conscious time to mulling the verse over and over in our minds and hearts. So many of us read it then say, 'Well I know that's true but I can't feel it.' The point is, the negative words have had years to sink in and wound our ability to feel. Our feelings often won't respond until we have received a truth in faith, so we need to keep speaking that truth to ourselves until it starts to bear fruit deep within us.

I discovered that passages like Psalm 139, Isaiah 61 and Zephaniah 3:17 were ones that God took me to many times. They were so rich with the character and love of God that I found my negative attitudes being transformed as I drank them in.

Another way is to meditate on a story where Jesus meets with some needy person, for example, the Samaritan woman in John 4. Instead of flicking over it thinking, 'I know this story . . .' stop and imagine what was really happening behind the bare outline. Put yourself in the shoes of the hurting person and then look at Jesus and see how He reacts. Hear the gentleness of His voice, see the kindness of His eyes. Let Him reach out and touch you.

I did this just the other day when I was trying to deal with a painful memory that would not go away. I asked God to speak to me and felt I should read the story of Jesus in the temple. As I meditated, I could almost see Jesus' anger and grief and His immediate action to transform the situation. Afterwards, He healed needy people in the same temple, touching them with gentleness and healing love. I imagined this scene while at the same time holding up to Him my own painful memory. As I 'saw' those poor, lame and blind people kneeling before Him in that temple and being touched by His gentle hand, I was able to imagine His hand stretched out in gentleness and healing to me too. I began to sense Him assuring me that my life was that temple and that He was always ready to act on my behalf to rescue me and to heal me.

Examples of Lives Changed through the Power of God's Word.

Because God is ultimately making us ready to reign with Him in heaven, He is constantly seeking to transform our minds and hearts so that we can be 'changed from one degree of glory to another' (2 Cor. 3:18 [Amplified Version]). We can often be in a state of turmoil or confusion or reacting angrily, sorrowfully or selfishly to some situation. That is where Jesus calls us to come and lay our burdens down before Him and listen. In that awesome moment when the disciples saw Jesus transfigured before them God said a very simple thing; 'Listen to Him!' God's ways are not our ways and if we truly want to grow deeper in our knowledge and love of God we need to listen to Him as we read His Word and to be willing to change if He seems to put the spotlight on some wrong attitude or show us a different way ahead. He will always reward us and give us joy as we humbly obey Him.

Do not Judge . . .

Marilyn was once very upset when on her birthday she went to house group only to be sat next to a man who lectured and preached at her throughout the whole evening. She went home fuming and poured out to her friend how this man had ruined her evening. Later on her friend suggested they do that day's Bible reading and Marilyn reluctantly agreed. They prayed that God would speak to them and then turned to the right page.

The first thing Marilyn read was, 'Do not judge or you too will be judged . . . ' (Matt. 7:1).

Marilyn gasped. She didn't want to hear that but she knew that God was speaking right into her heart. She was judging that man and felt she had a right to do so! There and then she prayed and asked God to change her heart and give her a new understanding of him. As she listened quietly God put the thought into her mind that he had recently had a breakdown which he was still working through and that he needed a lot of compassion and love.

The following week Marilyn went to her house group again and the same thing happened, she was put next to the man and again he preached at her all night. The difference was in Marilyn's response. Instead of getting frustrated and angry she really began to listen and realised that a lot of what he said was actually true. A love and respect for him filled her heart and when she got home she said how much she had enjoyed sitting next to him!

In this situation as Marilyn listened to God through His Word she was transformed more into His likeness.

Listening to Receive Forgiveness

People often have a problem in really believing and knowing that they are forgiven. But God's Word says clearly that there is no condemnation for those who are in Christ. We need, in faith, to take hold of that word of truth and use it as a weapon against our feelings of condemnation.

I remember one young man, Steven, who asked Marilyn and me to pray for him. 'I feel my Christian life has just dried up, as if there's a heavy weight on me,' he said.

Marilyn began to talk with him and under her gentle questioning he eventually opened up and revealed that he had had an affair with a married woman. Looking down in shame and covering his face with his hands his voice shook with sobs as he said, 'I keep asking God to forgive me but I don't see how He could. I was even going to church and singing hymns while I was doing that. He must hate me!'

'Steven,' said Marilyn softly, 'Jesus forgave you the very first time you asked!' He shook his head, still sobbing.

'Listen Steven, Jesus has forgiven you. It would be impossible for Him not to forgive you because it says in the Bible that He took all our sins onto Himself on the cross, not just some, but all!'

We read Steven different scriptures about God's forgiveness and then began to pray together. Quietly we welcomed the Holy Spirit and asked Him to give Steven real 'heart' understanding of God's forgiveness. Then Marilyn encouraged him, when he felt ready, to lay down his sin in front of the cross and accept Jesus' love and forgiveness.

After a long pause and with his head still bowed, Steven asked the Lord to forgive him. I then read out this verse: 'As far as the east is from the west, so far has He removed [your] transgressions from [you]. As a father has compassion on his children, so the Lord has compassion on [you] who fear Him' (Ps. 103:12–13).

Suddenly there was a bang. Startled, we looked up to see Steven standing with a broad smile on his face.

'It's gone, the weight's gone,' he cried. 'When you read that verse it lifted completely. I can feel God's love filling me, it's as if Jesus is sitting right there smiling at me.'

The power and the truth of God's Word ministered to Steven and broke down for ever those chains of self rejection and condemnation. Today he is a radiant Christian in love with his Lord.

Comfort in Bereavement

In 1993 our dearly loved pastor became ill with cancer. His family, our churches and many other local churches and individuals all began to seek God and pray for David's healing. He had such a wonderful ministry, it was inconceivable that he could die. When David was moved into a hospice his wife, Daphne, knew that humanly this meant that the end was near but she still clung on to the hope that God would heal him. One day as she was praying and reading the Bible this verse in Acts suddenly seemed to come alive to her, 'For when David had served God's purpose in his own generation . . . he was buried with his fathers' (Acts 13:36).

Daphne asked God to give her true understanding of what He was saying to her through this verse and in her own words this is what happened:

> The scripture prepared me and was part of the preparation that I was finding so difficult. I did release David and was privileged to be there when David died. There was a wonderful peace in the room . . . the scripture has brought me tremendous comfort since, to know that God was ultimately in charge of the timing of David's death . . . that He cared enough for me to reassure me that David had fulfilled his purposes . . . that has sustained me.

The Grace to Relinquish

God used a Bible verse to enable me to make a very difficult decision one year. I had been going out with Tim for about eight months and for a while everything was wonderful. Gradually, however, things started to change. We were so very different in our characters and in our vision of what we wanted to do with our lives. In the end we had a period of separation so that we could work out our feelings.

One night I cried out to God, 'Lord, please help me, I don't want to let him go, it hurts too much but I don't feel peaceful about carrying on either. Please speak to me!'

Suddenly a verse came to my mind about letting a grain of

wheat fall to the ground and die, and resulting in much fruit. I found a Bible and as I slowly read the verse it was as if it became imprinted on my heart and I knew that our relationship had to be like that grain of wheat, I had to let Tim go. With tears rolling down my cheeks I told God that I was willing to obey Him and I placed Tim and my feelings for him into God's hands. At that moment it was as if a wave of peace swept over me. All the pain and anguish in my heart lifted and I felt a depth of joy fill me.

That joy remained when I later heard that Tim also felt we should finish, and over the next few days it was as if I was carried in a covering of peace. Although this supernatural gift of grace lifted after a few days and I needed to keep working through the aftermath of the break up, I knew that something definite had happened in my heart as soon as I heard, trusted and obeyed God through His Word. When Tim later met Krissie and married her I felt nothing but joy for them.

Listening to Find our Way

One of the key areas where people worry about not hearing the Lord right and somehow getting out of the centre of His will, is guidance. We want to know what job we should be doing, what ministry we should be seeking to fulfil, what decisions we should be making in our day-to-day lives. Many of us run round in circles asking one person's advice after another but never really coming to any decision.

In 1982 Marilyn was approached by her record producer. She had made a couple of albums and had started singing at different venues at weekends.

'We think you should consider doing this work full time,' he said. 'Will you pray about it?'

Marilyn agreed to pray but was sure God would say no. She was shocked when she began to get a strong sense that God did want her to give up her teaching career for full-time ministry.

Over the next few weeks every obstacle but one was removed miraculously but the last one was a real barrier. Marilyn's parents were against her leaving the security of teaching and she did not want to take such a major step without their blessing. One day as she was praying about this she felt that she should read a certain verse in a Psalm. When she turned to it she was amazed to read, 'Listen, O daughter, consider and give ear: Forget your people and your father's house. The king is enthralled by your beauty; honour him, for he is your lord' (Ps. 45:10).

Marilyn did 'consider and give ear'. She knew this was God's Word to her and that she should obey Him rather than letting her parents make the decision. She laid down her desire for their blessing and made the decision to hand her notice in. That night her dad rang and said, 'Marilyn, we've realised this is a once in a lifetime opportunity for you and we don't want to hold you back. We want you to know that if you go ahead we will be behind you.'

As soon as Marilyn heard and sacrificially obeyed what God was telling her through His Word, God worked on her behalf to bring about the very thing she had desired.

Listening – to Become like Him

I believe that God will guide us, both in the major decisions and in the 'nitty gritty' details of everyday life. God says He knows the plans He has for us and that He has already prepared for us the works He wants us to do (Ephesians 2:10). But I feel that while we seek God for direction in our jobs, relationships etc., we should also be holding in balance the ultimate purposes that God has for us in making us His beloved sons and daughters. The most important thing we can 'do' as Christians is to grow in our knowledge and love of God and to become like Him. Becoming like Him means reaching out to others with the same costly forgiving love as He does. Suppose we 'listen' to God's guidance, start in a perfect job but have too hard hearts to reach out to the people we work with? Would we have really heard God? Maybe it could even be better to go through a period of unemployment to enable us to have the time to learn to be still before God, to hear His still small voice and to receive His compassion for others rather than rushing straight into work.

Why we Seek to Listen to God Through the Bible

God is not an agony aunt who we contact every now and then to give us some solution to a problem and then forget. He is the Almighty Creator of this universe who is holding all things together and is working all things out to their awesome fulfilment. In His Word He has given us pictures, clear warnings and symbolic messages all drawing us to know Him and to be running with Him as His plans are unfolded. That is why we need to be reading and studying His Word regularly and systematically, so that we can develop a full 'heart' picture of what God is saying to us. I have mentioned several occasions where God has led myself or others to a particularly helpful verse, but that has usually happened whilst in the course of a regular reading, rather than just opening the Bible and hoping to find something appropriate, like a magic book. As Paul declares to Timothy, '*All scripture is God breathed* and is useful for teaching, rebuking, correcting and training in righteousness, so that the man of God may be thoroughly equipped for every good work' (2 Tim. 3:16, italics mine).

The Joy of Knowing God

Jesus said, 'Now this is eternal life: that they may know you, the only true God, and Jesus Christ whom you have sent' (John 17:3).

Jesus knew His Father God in a way that no man has before or since. Even as a boy He was willing to endure His parents' anger in order to be able to spend some more time in the temple, sitting at the Rabbi's feet, hearing the Word of God and learning more about His Father. He knew the Scriptures intimately but His was not just a knowledge for its own sake but a knowledge that drew Him heart to heart, mind to mind, spirit to spirit with His Father. In all His words and prayers He expressed deep intimacy with His Father and sought to draw others into that same place.

Jesus has called us to reach this world for Him, to embrace lonely hurting people with His love, to stand against the immorality and injustice of our times, to feed those that are hungry and in need. He has called us to be fruitful in every way for Him. We can do all this, not by frantically rushing round trying to achieve the world, but by taking time to sit at His feet, drinking in His words, listening to Him, loving Him and so becoming like Him.

As Marilyn's song puts it:

Sitting at His feet, that's where I long to be.
Drawing close to Him, more of His heart I see.
Listening to His Word, obeying what I've heard
Opening my life to Him in every part.
Letting Him be my goal, letting Him take control
So He can change me and make me all He wants me to be.[4]

OVER TO YOU

1 Give yourself a period of time, say half an hour where you can be quiet with God. Sit quietly for a few moments in a relaxed position. Thank the Lord that He is with you and wants to speak to you. If there are any immediate worries or burdens on your mind consciously lift them up to God and leave them with Him.
2 Ask the Holy Spirit to come as your friend and teacher. Ask

Him to open up the Bible to you as you read it. Imagine Him sitting next to you pointing out the different verses.

3 Read Psalm 103:1–5 slowly, taking each phrase, thinking what it means, allowing yourself to feel the truth of it, making it your own prayer or song of praise. Think of what it reveals to you of God's character and allow Him to speak into any needs you have and touch you with His love.

4 Read Luke 19:1–10. Put yourself into Zacchaeus's shoes, talk through these questions with Jesus and give Him time to speak to you.
   - How do you feel knowing there are those wrong things in your life but still wanting to see Jesus?
   - Are there times when like him you hide yourself because you fear rejection?
   - How do you feel when Jesus looks straight at you?
   - How do you expect Him to speak to you?
   - How do you feel when you realise He wants to spend time with you, to talk with you, to eat with you, to be part of your life?
   - Look at Zacchaeus's heartfelt response to Jesus' love. Is there any way you need to respond to Jesus?

4
Listening Through Creation and Everyday Life

Glimpses of God

One day I was having my eyes tested. Peter, the optician, a Christian friend of mine, peered into the back of my eyes with his special light, then rose, put the main lights on again and smiled at me.

'That's it for now, then,' he said. 'No change at present.'

Just as I was getting my bags, Peter said thoughtfully, 'You know, if I hadn't already been a Christian, I would have known there was a God of love just by looking at the eye and seeing how it works.'

He went on to explain the intricate and wonderful workings of the eye and the process of seeing that had led him to that conclusion. But it was the simplicity of his first statement that really caught my attention. Peter had been deeply touched with the reality and power of God's love through something that most of us take completely for granted. This wasn't words in a book describing God and persuading people to believe in Him. This was an ordinary man undertaking an ordinary job and through that receiving a lasting message from God.

On another occasion I had a friend, Rosie, round for dinner. As we washed up afterwards she started sharing about her feelings of worthlessness compared to other Christians.

'None of them seem to have made the kind of mistakes I have,' she said sadly. 'I just don't see how God is going to be able to use me in my life.'

I was silent for a moment, wondering how to answer. I knew it would be useless to say that she needed to stop comparing herself to others and just accept God's forgiveness for herself. I continued scrubbing hard at the greasy pan while I was thinking. Suddenly an amazing thought occurred to me and I burst out laughing. She looked at me, startled.

'Sorry Rosie,' I said, 'I'm not laughing at you! This thought suddenly came to me about the washing up! God seemed to say: "You have to wash up everything, whether it is just a plate with a few crumbs on or a greasy meat tin, it all has to go through the same process of washing up otherwise it will stay dirty! In the same way everyone has to be washed clean by my precious blood, whether in their eyes they've committed few or many sins. They all equally need my forgiveness!"'

Rosie stared at me. 'I suppose that means I shouldn't worry about everyone else but just accept what God has done for me?'

I nodded and suddenly she laughed and said, 'I bet I was that greasy meat tin!' She held it up to the light as she dried it. 'It's lovely and sparkly now it's been cleaned isn't it?'

I was thrilled to see that there was a new sparkle in her eyes too.

Look at the Stars

At my baptism, five weeks after my conversion, a prophecy was given to me emphasising God's longing to communicate, 'I will speak to you what is on my heart for you and for those that are near you . . . because I the Lord delight in revealing my secrets to those who love me . . .'

Although I thought this prophecy had lovely words I did not really understand it. I thought that you could only hear God through reading the Bible and hearing others teaching it. As I couldn't hear any sermons I felt that my understanding of God would fully depend on what I learnt myself from the Bible. It took the wise suggestion of my pastor, one night at church, to ignite my understanding that God wanted to talk to me through many other means. It started a search that has grown ever more rewarding and illuminating.

All around me in the crowded church, people were singing and worshipping.

I wasn't. I couldn't. The words were beautiful and the music full of tenderness. I really tried to sing with the others but I knew that I was just mouthing the words, they had no real meaning to me. As I looked again at their faces, I felt a deep sense of sadness. What was wrong with me that I could not enter into the worship like everyone else? Why was my heart so hard and so unwilling to believe? I sank down into my chair and buried my face in my hands. I did not want to see the words any more or to hear them.

Sometime later I felt a hand on my shoulder. Slowly, I raised my head and looked up at David, my pastor. He smiled at me and spoke gently.

'What's happening, Tracy?'

'I can't join in like everyone else. None of it seems real to me.' I began to cry.

David did not answer for a while but stayed quietly by my side, then he said, 'What you really mean, Tracy, is that you can't believe God loves you, isn't it?'

I considered his words for a while and then nodded.

'Yes, I suppose that's true,' I said. 'I know in my head that He loves me, but in my heart I just can't feel His love. I just don't know how I could mean anything to Him.'

David began to share some verses of the Bible about God's love. I listened but although mentally I was assenting to all he said, I still could not feel the truth of it. After a while David stopped and looking at me thoughtfully, smiled and said, 'It's still not going in, is it Tracy? Listen,' he paused and put his hand on my arm. 'I will pray with you in the week, but in the meantime I want you to do some homework. I want you to go home, and when it is dark go outside and look at the stars.'

I stared at him. 'Look at the stars? What do I want to do that for?'

He laughed. 'I'm not telling you any more. Just do as I said.'

That night as soon as it was dark I carried out David's suggestion. I let myself out of the back door of the hostel I lived in and began to wander randomly across the fields.

It was a warm night and very still. As I walked I was aware that I still felt very churned up inside and the darkness and isolation of the night were oppressing me. This was a stupid idea! I thought, kicking at the grass. What was David thinking of when he told me to do this?

Suddenly the weight of the loneliness I was feeling overwhelmed me. Forgetting the nearby hostel and the possibility of passers by, I stopped, and gazing angrily into the blackness of the sky, cried out to God.

'Well who am I then? Are you there? Do you really love me?'

Panting with the force of the emotion within me, I stopped. The clamour of my words resounded around me and then faded away into silence. The stillness returned.

For a moment, I almost expected an audible reply but there was none. I stood staring at the sky, the heat of my anger draining away as I waited silently. Somehow I knew that God was going to speak to me.

As I gazed into the blackness it seemed that all my inner darkness and pain was revealed there. I felt a complete nothingness within and nothingness was all this night sky seemed to contain. Then my eye was drawn to a tiny twinkling light in the middle of that blackness. It was a star! Then I saw another and another and another . . . each one so tiny, yet each with the power to push back the encircling darkness with the brightness of its light. I gazed from one to the other in wonder. It was as if

I'd never seen them before, as if I'd only ever been aware of the darkness, ignoring the vastness and brightness of the universe to which the darkness was just a backdrop.

As I gazed at them I prayed silently.

'Lord Jesus, what do you want to teach me through these stars? What was it David wanted me to see?'

I continued looking upwards. It was amazing to me how alive the night sky now appeared to be. I marvelled at the variety in size and shape, brightness and movement that even I with my limited vision could perceive now that I was really looking. I felt very small in contrast to this revealed vastness of creation, but strangely I no longer found that frightening. Suddenly some words came into my mind which I recognised as being from the Bible.

> When I consider your heavens, the work of your fingers, the moon and the stars, which you have set in place, what is man that you are mindful of him, the son of man that you care for him? You made him a little lower than the heavenly beings and crowned him with glory and honour. (Ps. 8:3–5)

In the stillness of that night God seemed to speak right into my heart. I sensed that He was telling me that even as he had poured out His creative love and power into the universe, creating the stars, giving each their individual stamp of beauty and setting each in its assigned place, so in even greater measure He had done the same for me. For I was not just a created 'thing', but someone who was 'just a little lower than the heavenly beings'! Even as He knew each star and each had its own individual beauty so He knew and loved me and I too was in my assigned place where I could best shine out for Him.

From my heart I whispered to Him,

'Thank you Father that in all your immensity and power you know me and love me and I belong to you.'

As David had foreseen, God had spoken into my need. Not through human words of comfort but through His own language – His creation – in this case, the stars.

God is not Limited

These are just examples of the exciting truth that as our Father, God loves to communicate in many different ways with His children. The Bible itself shows the breadth and immensity of the ways God has chosen to speak to us. From the earliest chapters of Genesis through to the prophetic visions of Revelation it is full of examples of God speaking, and revealing His heart and purposes to individuals in ways apart from Scripture, that each could understand.

He Speaks Through Creation

Since that milestone night I have learnt more and more that God made this world to be as His letter to mankind. The Bible is full of joyful praise that God expresses Himself to man through creation. 'The heavens declare the glory of God; the skies proclaim the work of His hands. Day after day they pour forth speech; night after night they display knowledge' (Ps. 19:1–2).

He gave Abraham the promise of a son and heir, again through the stars. He sealed His covenant with Noah through a rainbow. He called Moses through a burning bush. From the smallest daisy to the magnificent mountain ranges each has been created to speak to us of Him. That is why it declares in Romans 1 'Since the creation of the worlds God's invisible qualities – His eternal power and divine nature – have been clearly seen, being understood from what has been made . . .' (Rom. 1:20).

Many of the Psalms focus on the things in nature to draw man's heart in worship to God. For example, the whole of Psalm 104 expresses the writer's understanding that God

Almighty has not only created but has provided for the needs of every living thing. As he meditates on these things his heart soars with praise to God.

> O Lord my God, you are very great; you are clothed with splendour and majesty . . . How many are your works, O Lord! In wisdom you made them all; . . . I will sing to the Lord all my life; I will sing praise to my God as long as I live . . . Praise the Lord, O my soul. Praise the Lord. (Ps. 104:1, 24, 33–5)

I realised as I read more deeply in the Old Testament that these psalmists were not men living relaxed, peaceful lives with plenty of time for mystical contemplation, but were experiencing great hardship and sometimes constant danger and betrayal. Yet within that, and despite that, they were moved to hear and love God as they saw the evidence of His love through the things He had made. In Psalm 121, the writer is obviously in trouble and while taking a walk, starts to look about him as he prays. 'I lift up my eyes to the hills – where does my help come from? My help comes from the Lord, the Maker of heaven and earth' (Ps. 121:1–2).

As he physically looks away from himself and up to the surrounding hills he becomes aware of the greatness of God and realises that if God made heaven and earth He is certainly big enough to help him. The remainder of the Psalm is full of the confidence that the writer has found from looking at the hills that God is in control of every part of his life.

It is recorded that Brother Lawrence, a seventeenth-century monk who through his writings *Practising the Presence of God* has inspired thousands, became a Christian as he gazed at the bare branches of a tree in winter. He was overwhelmed by the sudden awareness of God's regenerative love symbolised by the tree as it passed through the changing seasons. His life was transformed through that simple action of taking time to listen to God through the natural world.

Jesus said very little directly about Himself or God in comparison with the amount of teaching that was in the form of stories and parables drawn from creation and everyday life. When He was surrounded by a group of disciples who were worried and anxious about the future, He did not shout, 'Why don't you have more faith?' but simply pointed to the wild flowers and the birds, graphically bringing home the fact that if God loved a simple flower that much, how much more would He provide for His children?

Listening Through Everyday Life

Jesus constantly communicated the truths of God to the crowds that followed Him everywhere. His words were pithy, powerful and so incredibly authoritative that even those who were against Him were stunned into silence. And yet they were simple everyday illustrations from everyday life. As He walked from place to place, from town to country, from desert to lakeside, He was keenly aware of everything that was happening around Him. Building, farming, fishing, bread-making, relationships, jewels – anything was a possible medium for God to speak through. He looked, listened and experienced everything with His normal human senses, at the same time talking to God His Father and receiving deep spiritual insights.

The Parable of the Sower, for example, would have been something most people would have immediately identified with. They would have known from bitter daily experience that only a small percentage of the seed so painstakingly sown would actually bear fruit. But Jesus was talking about something much deeper than mere farming procedures. He was pointing to their own level of responsiveness to Him. He knew that by identifying the message of the kingdom of God with their experience of daily life they would have something much more pointed and real to respond to than if He had simply said, 'Seek God'; 'Respond fully to God'; 'Build your lives on the foundations of faith.'

Jesus said many times to the crowds surrounding Him, 'He who has ears to hear, let him hear.' So often they heard on the surface only, mere hearing without true listening to the message in His words. And yet it was said of Him that the parables He spoke would be the means by which He would reveal the very deep things of God. '"I will open my mouth in parables, I will utter things hidden since the creation of the world"' (Matt. 13:35).

What Jesus said then, remains true for us today. If He spoke then through ordinary things and expected people to hear the spiritual lesson behind them, He will do the same now.

He will Speak Through our Everyday Lives too

So many of us feel guilty because our lives are forced to go at such a hectic pace we don't give much time to God. We then often squash Him into a little slot of 'religious activity' when He has been with us all day longing to speak to us within our normal lives.

The truth of this came to me afresh a few months ago when I was eating some toast. We were in a hurry to leave to do some concerts and I was trying to eat quickly. My throat was a bit sore and I found it hard to swallow the crusts which had got burnt. In the end I pushed them to the side of my plate and just ate the softer, middle part. Suddenly this mundane action seemed significant.

'Lord, are you trying to speak to me through this?' I prayed silently. Back came this thought:

> 'When you read my Word you are only responding to the parts that you like to hear! Anything that makes you feel a bit uncomfortable you run away from and therefore don't

take in. But just as the crusts on that toast are as equally nutritious as the rest of the "more easy-to-chew" parts, so it is important for you to have the "harder-to-chew" parts of my Word, otherwise you will miss out on all I want to do for you.'

I was amazed and amused by the accuracy of this thought! It was true that those areas of the Bible which seemed to point more to wrong attitudes that I needed to change I tended to quickly skim over, preferring to spend time meditating on a nice passage about God's love for me. I laughed as I realised that it had taken two discarded crusts for God to reveal what was happening.

A similar thing happened when I was on my way to Poland with Marilyn. I had never been there before and was feeling excited about it all. We were having dinner – roast chicken. I happened to have the wishbone on my plate which I put to one side. I then carried on eating and chatting with the others. A thought began to grow in my mind that was quite separate to anything that was being said. Rather startled I said to God, 'Lord do you want me to hear something from you?' I tried to distance my mind from all that was going on around me and tune into God instead and gradually the thought took shape:

'Tracy, when you used to pull that wishbone as a child, you enjoyed the excitement and if you got the right end you would make your wish. But you never really believed that it would come true, you knew it was just a game. That is how you have been praying to me recently! You've made your requests and expressed your wishes and needs, but deep down you haven't believed I would answer. But I am not a wishbone! I am God! I am your loving Heavenly Father and I want to answer your prayers. If only you will believe that and come to me with real faith and expectancy you will see them answered.'

Once again I was dumbfounded. It was true but I would never have realised that was happening. At the beginning of my Christian life I had been full of enthusiasm to pray but gradually it had become more of a ritual than a reality. This word through the wishbone really shook me out of that and forced me to face up to my lack of faith and trust in my Heavenly Father. If I find myself going into a rut again now I always catch myself by thinking 'wishbone'!

On both these occasions God broke in on my thoughts quite unexpectedly. I am coming to believe that God longs to be able to do that at all times for all of us. If you are chatting with a friend you may be talking about one thing and then she will suddenly go off at a tangent and start talking about something else. Jesus said that we are His sheep and His sheep know and listen to His voice (John 10:1–5). The sheep may all be roaming contentedly around the pasture when they suddenly hear their shepherd's voice calling them and they leave their grazing and turn to follow him. That was what was happening with me. I was doing something, my mind elsewhere, but when God put those thoughts into my mind I recognised them as being from Him and turned my thoughts to Him to hear what He wanted to say.

In the book of Acts chapter 10:9–23 Peter is shown to have a similar experience. He goes up on the rooftop to pray. He is hungry and therefore probably quite distracted by thoughts of food while he is praying. It is that very thing that God uses to speak to him in an incredible way. He shows him a vision of all kinds of unclean animals that Peter was to 'kill and eat'. Each time Peter protests on the basis of them being impure God says, 'Do not call anything impure that God has made clean.'

The upshot of God speaking to Peter in this way was that because the previously unclean food was now to be seen as clean, the Gentiles were now also to be seen as clean. The nature of evangelism was permanently transformed and the whole world instead of a tiny community was to be reached with the gospel.

How do we Know when it is God?

Many of us worry because we fear we will not know how to hear God through these means. Suppose the thoughts are not from God at all? Suppose I am just imagining things? Isn't it all getting a bit too experiential to expect to hear Almighty God through anything and everything?

I am learning that it is an ongoing process to learn to listen to God in this way. I consciously give my mind to Him and thank Him that He has given me the mind of Christ. I usually do that first thing in the morning and I ask Him at the same time to fill me in every part of my being with His Holy Spirit. When I read the Bible I expect Him to make it alive to me and then when I continue through my day I keep trying to turn my thoughts towards Him, asking Him to come close to me and speak to me through whatever means He wants to.

Because of the work I do as Marilyn's personal assistant, quite a few of our days each week are spent doing concerts. On these days I try to tune in to God in a two-fold way, firstly to hear Him for myself and secondly to hear Him for the people who will be at the concert.

On one occasion I was in a church vestry just before a concert. Both Marilyn and I had been praying, trying to get a sense of what God wanted to say at this particular event. Neither of us felt we knew very clearly, even though it was now nearly time for the concert to begin. All we felt as we prayed was a sense of heaviness but we didn't know why. Some of the church leaders joined us to pray. I happened to glance abstractedly at the carpet. It was one of those thick pile carpets where if you brush it the wrong way, the pile shows up as a dark streak. This carpet had such a streak in it and it suddenly seemed to become very significant, in a similar way to how a Bible verse might do. I asked the Lord if there was anything He was trying to tell me and this thought came to my mind:

> 'I have called my people to flow together in love and harmony so that the world may see what I am like. But this church has become divided because of resentments, gossip and criticism. That division is becoming obvious to outsiders, just like the streak in a carpet becomes obvious.'

Rather hesitantly, I shared this thought during the concert. I was very worried that I may have got it wrong and would offend the people there, but I sensed an urgency that it needed to be said. It may have been that it did offend some, but I was very moved and glad I had spoken when some came to me at the end, including a leader, and said that God had spoken to them through it and they had repented.

The way God spoke to me through that streak in the carpet was a little like how He spoke to Jeremiah through a potter (Jer. 18:1–5). Jeremiah was busy doing something when he had a strong sense that he should go and watch the potter at work. Seeing him shape a marred pot into a new design, Jeremiah suddenly became aware that God was using this ordinary incident to speak a powerful prophetic message to the house of Israel!

Catching the Tail

In practice, I find that I often don't know for sure if a sudden thought is going to be from God until I've given it back to Him and asked Him to make it more real and meaningful. I call this 'catching the tail' of the thought or idea and I use this principle for many aspects of listening to God, not just this one.

This is what I mean. If you are walking in the woods and you see an animal's tail sticking out of a hole and you want to discover what it is you would have to catch hold of the tail and then dig the hole a bit deeper in order for the whole animal to be unearthed. In the same way, when God starts to speak to us it is often by slightly drawing our attention to something. That is the 'tail'. To leave it there is not enough to disclose whether or not it is from God, let alone the fullness of what He might be wanting to say. So then we need to 'dig deeper'. This means giving it back to Him and asking Him to confirm it and give a full picture of it. I usually pray something like 'Lord, this . . . seems meaningful. Is it from you Lord? What do you want me to know? . . .'

Then I wait. It is very easy for us to presume we know the answer but it needs to come from Him. If there is the possibility that it may be something to share in a concert or for an individual I ask Him to give me a real sense of peace before I say anything.

Mistakes!

I have made mistakes many times and still do. There are times when I just can't be bothered to tune in to God, I've just got too much to do! On other occasions I've presumed that because God has revealed something once that it will be right to bring the same theme again and again.

On one occasion I'd been admiring someone's patchwork quilt and thinking how lovely it was that the different squares harmonised so beautifully into the quilt's pattern. The thought came to me that there was going to be someone there that night whose life had been ripped apart by tragic circumstances and who felt she could never be whole again. God seemed to say that even as in the quilt the odd little fragments of unmatched colour were joined together to form a harmonious whole, so for this person, He was going to join the broken fragments of her life together and make her a new person healed and whole and alive with His colour and beauty. A lady responded. She had been very touched by the picture and we were able to pray for God to start that healing work in her.

The problem was, I liked the idea of this word! So the next night I brought it again at another concert. This time it was a rug not a quilt. The next time it was a vase and then a jug! It wasn't until Marilyn said to me that night, 'Trace, I've never heard of a patchwork jug in my life before!' that I realised what I'd done! Needless to say, the word was only responded to the very first night!

Not Just 'Up-front' People

People often say that because they are leading humdrum lives, in ordinary jobs or as housewives or unemployed, they are not 'up front' like me and therefore this kind of listening would not be appropriate for them, because they wouldn't have anyone to share with like I do.

To God nothing and no one is humdrum. It is true that during the concerts Marilyn and I are on a stage but we are just ordinary people. The main part of my work for Marilyn is helping her run her house, going shopping with her, doing the ordinary things that make up life. It is in those perfectly ordinary, mundane things that can make our day so busy and yet leave us feeling we've done nothing, that I am learning to lift my mind up to God instead of just drifting aimlessly, or even give the aimless drifting to Him and ask Him to bless it and direct it and show me something of Himself through it.

Our sound engineer, Paul, had never experienced God speaking in this kind of way before. After I'd been sharing some of these thoughts in a workshop one day, he went back to his room and asked God to speak to Him through something there. As he prayed quietly he looked around him and noticed that while he had organised things very tidily in one part of the room, in another part his things were scattered around. God told Paul that he need not fear and try to hide the parts of his inner life that were not 'sorted out' yet. God could see both the parts of his life that were 'tidy' and those that were 'untidy' but He loved and accepted him as he was and was working with him to make him the kind of person he wanted to be.

This simple encouragement from the Lord, through his room, gave Paul the confidence to keep seeking Him and now he is growing in his ability to hear God for others as well as himself.

At another workshop, a young girl went outside and prayed that God would speak to her through something in the gardens. She sat down on a log and a sharp piece of bark jabbed her leg! She was about to move to a different spot when she sensed that it was through this very piece of bark that God wanted to speak to her. As she sat quietly He began to reveal different areas of her life where she was like that bark, sharp and hurtful at times to other people. God seemed to say very lovingly, 'If you allow me to take care of those hurts and bitter memories in your life instead of holding on to them, I will make you beautiful and full of the depth and intricacy of the bark, but without its sharp edges!'

She repented and when she shared this, that beauty was already shining out of her.

OVER TO YOU

Some of us respond more to nature. Some to normal everyday things, maybe associated with life in the town, their house or room, the things they do at work or at home. Others may like to think of childhood memories, meals, parties, school etc. We are all different so just use a way that seems most comfortable to you. Get a notebook and pen ready to jot down anything.

1 Start by thanking the Lord that you are His child and therefore can come to Him trustingly and expect Him to want to speak to you.

2 Thank Him that He has given you the mind of Christ and the gift of His Holy Spirit. Ask Him to fill every part of you and to make the thoughts and love of God alive and real. Thank Him that He will do this.
3 Choose one of the above areas that seems natural to you. The following are just a few suggestions for each area but of course you could use anything you like!

a) If you are a nature person:

- Go into your garden and look at the trees, flowers, sky, any birds or animals. What effect is the season having on the different things? Is the sun shining or are there clouds? What happens to the grass that is crushed under your feet? Look slowly, using all your senses, either at the whole or concentrating on one small flower or bird. Look at the colours, the design, the way the different parts work together.

  One frail old lady in a workshop was deeply encouraged as she looked at a tiny sparrow on a fence. She remembered Jesus' loving words relating to sparrows and was able to trust Him afresh to look after her in her frailty.
- As you look and meditate ask the Lord if He wants to speak to you. If you have any pressing needs or worries be honest with Him about them and ask Him to speak into them. If you don't get any specific thoughts don't worry! Just allow the awareness of God's love in His creation to lift your heart in worship to Him.

b) If you are a 'things' person:

- Go into a room in your house that is personal to you. Look around slowly. Notice things like how organised it is. How light is it? Are curtains open or closed? Are there things in it that obviously display your character or is it quite impersonal? As you look, ask God to speak into your life and needs. Are there curtains of fear or shame shutting out the light of His love in your life? Are you putting on an impersonal front and keeping the 'real you' safely tidied away? Talk to Him about any thoughts or ideas that come to your mind as you look around.

- Get on with doing something that needs doing but ask God to speak to you through your job or task, e.g., cleaning, typing, filing etc. Just the other day I was doing some ironing and was feeling a bit down because I knew that I'd upset someone. I found my mind was futilely going over and over the situation so without much expectation I asked God if there was anything He wanted to say to me. These thoughts came into my mind:

  'You are taking so much care to make sure that this blouse looks its best. You are gentle with it but at the same time you can see exactly what needs to be done. You see with your mind's eye how perfectly it will come out. My child, I am treating you in the same way. I love you dearly and am therefore gentle with you even while I am working on those areas that need to be changed. I don't see you as a mess but already perfect because I know what I am making you.'

  I finished that ironing with much more enthusiasm than when I'd started and that simple thought lifted my spirits through the rest of that day.

- If your mind drifts around and you find it hard to concentrate, let it drift! But ask the Lord to direct it or speak to you through any particular thoughts or memories. A group of children caught my attention one day. I found myself reliving memories of childhood parties where I had always felt the odd one out. I was about to drift on to another thought when I sensed God was saying that He wanted me to describe that party scene in a concert, pointing out that He had no favourites and loved to be with and talk with all His children and has a special love for all those who feel alone! A young lady responded who had felt very isolated and rejected, especially at social gatherings!

Don't worry if nothing comes at first! Remember it's taken me a few years to learn and put all these ideas into practice. Often weeks can go by where I don't hear anything or I make mistakes in what I do hear. Then something brings God's voice alive to me afresh and it's like finding a jewel! It is worth persevering when it's treasure you're seeking. So keep going!

5
Unwrapping His Gifts

Divinely Inspired Knowledge

'You look awful,' Marilyn's friend said, 'aren't you well?'

'No,' said Marilyn, 'I get these terrible pains in my stomach. I've had them for years but the doctors can't find anything wrong!'

'Shall we pray about it?'

'I'm sick of praying!' Marilyn exclaimed. 'It just gets worse!'

'But have you ever asked God to show you the root?'

'Well, no, not really . . .'

'Well let's just ask Him then,' her friend said, drawing her chair up.

They prayed silently then she spoke again.

'Were you ever in an oxygen tent?'

'Yes I was a premature baby.'

'Well, I've got this picture of you in this tent as a tiny baby. I sense you feel very lonely and afraid and you are missing your mum. I think we need to pray that God will take away the fear and loneliness and assure you of His loving presence with you. Are you happy to do that?'

'Yes,' Marilyn said, rather doubtfully.

Her friend prayed but Marilyn felt nothing except a slight sense of peace. She was still in pain. The next day she got up, went to work (she was a teacher then) came home, cooked dinner and suddenly realised she hadn't had a pain. Maybe it was just a good day, she thought. Next day, no pain. Day after, no pain. She has never had one since!

When Marilyn reflected on this she realised that the pains had started when she was sent away from home to go to boarding school, but she never had them in the holidays. That enforced separation had ignited the long buried fear and loneliness from her birth experience and set off the pains. Through this picture God revealed an emotional root which when prayed for led to her being physically healed.

God Gives us Knowledge – the Biblical Proof

Hearing about this incident and others like it, I felt a deep sense of awe. On each occasion it was just an ordinary person hearing something from God which they could not possibly have known themselves. Could it be that hearing Him in this way was something we are all meant to experience? I began to read the Bible with new eyes, looking for any passages where people were given that same kind of supernatural knowledge.

I found that God spoke again and again in the Old Testament through dreams, visions, symbolic pictures, and specific words to people who were open to His voice. Then in the New Testament Jesus came as the highest of all prophets. He knew without being told, what people were thinking and planning. He spoke accurately into their needs whether they were spiritual, emotional or purely physical. He revealed supernatural knowledge about people and situations, He healed the sick, discerned evil spirits and cast them out. He raised the dead, took a miraculous authority over the natural world and prophesied of things that would take place in future days.

Near the end of His life Jesus told the disciples, 'Anyone who has faith in me will do what I have been doing. He will do even greater things than these, because I am going to the Father' (John 14:12).

That promise started to be fulfilled on the day of Pentecost when the disciples were filled with the Holy Spirit. As I read what happened next in Acts, I was overwhelmed at the sheer number of times they were shown hidden things through visions, words of knowledge, dreams, and prophecies. As they listened and obeyed God's voice, His power was released, resulting in healings, conversions, individuals changing the direction of their lives and most of all, the kingdom of God being dramatically extended.

I also read in Joel, 'I will pour out my Spirit on all people. Your sons and daughters will prophesy, your old men will dream dreams, your young men will see visions. Even on my servants, both men and women, I will pour out my Spirit in those days' (Joel 2:28–9).

I was amazed when I discovered these very same verses quoted again in Acts and realised that Peter was declaring that this prophecy was fulfilled at Pentecost and from then on '*now*' is the time for the ordinary folk, the men and women, young and old, me and you, to be hearing God in supernatural ways, not just the leaders but 'all people . . .'

Some other verses in 1 Corinthians brought this home all the more. It says that to each one the manifestation of the Spirit is given for the common good. To one there is given through the Spirit the message of wisdom, to another the message of knowledge, to another faith, gifts of healing, miraculous powers, prophecy, distinguishing between spirits, speaking in different kinds of tongues and the interpretation of tongues (1 Cor. 12:4–10 adapted).

These verses simply said 'to each one . . . is given', it seemed so matter of fact and I began to understand that it really is God's desire and intention that we all hear Him in this way, that it is His gift to each one of us. I so longed to be able to hear God like this myself. I remembered the prophecy I was given at my baptism and I began to pray, 'O Lord, please give me a heart that's in tune with yours and ears that are open to your smallest whisper.'

My First Word of Knowledge

I was on a young people's weekend when one of the leaders had a prophecy for an individual who consciously needed to stop running and make the decision to commit themselves to God. No one responded and after a while the meeting ended.

As I went upstairs I prayed quietly that whoever it was for would be able to respond. A girl passed me just as I reached my door and suddenly a voice seemed to say inside me, 'This is the person.' I was shocked! Was I just imagining things? Then another thought seemed to take shape within me. 'Tell her that she needs to let go of her boyfriend because he won't give her the happiness she is looking for and is standing in the way of her coming to me!'

By now I was shaking! I couldn't possibly say that to her! 'Lord, I can hardly remember what she looked like and I don't even know her name!'

Just then someone came round the corner at the end of the corridor and with disbelief I recognised the girl!

'Can I just have a word?' I asked diffidently.

'Yes, what is it?'

'Well I felt God might be saying that prophecy was for you.' I paused but she didn't say anything so I blundered on. 'He seemed to say, you need to give your boyfriend up because he is stopping you finding the happiness that only God can give you!'

There it was out! I looked down at the floor expecting a torrent of angry words and was startled when I heard her saying quietly, 'Can we talk?'

We talked for two hours then went to bed. The following evening I was full of joy when I saw her go forward at the end of the meeting to become a Christian.

In *The Holy Spirit and You* Dennis and Rita Bennett describe the gifts as follows:

> The word of knowledge is the supernatural revelation of facts past, present or future which were not learned through the

> efforts of the natural mind. It may be described as the Mind of Christ being manifested in the mind of the believer and is given when needed in a flash of time . . . The gift of prophecy is manifested when believers speak the mind of God by the inspiration of the Holy Spirit and not from their own thoughts. It is supernatural speech in a known language.[1]

That was what had happened with me. A sudden awareness, both of her situation and God's heart for her which was expressed in the prophecy.

Ask and Receive

Many people say, 'Well I know what the gifts are but I don't know how to receive them!'

A friend of mine, Penny, once gave me a money gift to buy a new coat. I needed the coat but when she put the cheque in my hands I felt awful. All I could think of were the times I'd failed and let her or other people down. I refused the gift because I felt so unworthy and of course, I really hurt Pen. Later Marilyn talked to me and pointed out that Pen just wanted to give it to me because she loved me and wasn't even thinking about whether I deserved it or not. I apologised to Pen and when she offered the cheque again, received it with thanks. I will never forget the look of joy on her face and it made me realise how much joy it must give God when we receive His gifts.

The spiritual gifts are called that because they are God's presents to us. We cannot get them in any other way than by receiving them from His loving hand, just like we receive presents from each other at Christmas. Often when it comes round to December, I say to my Mum, 'I'd love a new blouse or some earrings' and then on Christmas Day I receive what I have asked for.

I found a wonderful verse about asking in Matthew that

really brought home to me the extent to which our Father God longs to respond to our childlike trust,

> Which of you, if his son asks for bread, will give him a stone? Or if he asks for fish, will give him a snake? If you, then, though you are evil, know how to give good gifts to your children, how much more will your Father in heaven give good gifts to those who ask Him! (Matt. 7:9–11)

Often we feel too unworthy as Christians to claim to have received a spiritual gift and so we just keep on asking. But God says His love for us is unlimited. He wants to give to us, not because we are good enough but just because He is our 'Daddy' and He loves us.

We Must be Praying

The other side of the coin to asking and receiving, is our need to be praying. Jesus said many times, 'He who has ears to hear let him hear.' We cannot have ears to hear unless we are praying, talking and listening to God, bringing our thoughts and hearts in tune with His. Seeking Him for those we love who are struggling or in need in some way. Praying for our neighbourhood or nation or our unsaved family or colleagues. Jesus always reveals His heart to those who seek Him but never just to gratify our need for importance.

The other Sunday I was in my church with my friend Debra. Suddenly, Rachel, our pastor's wife came up and started talking to her. It turned out that Debra had been very ill the week before with an ear infection and had to take time off work. Rachel had been praying for the church during the week and kept getting a strong feeling that Debra was in pain. She prayed a great deal for her all through that week but it wasn't until the Sunday that her impression was confirmed. Debra's ear infection improved quickly and it was a real comfort for her to know that when she had been feeling so awful, God had told someone to pray for her.

Rachel had not been praying specifically for Debra at first, just the church as a whole. But the point is, she *was* praying and because she was praying she was open to God and able to hear His voice when He spoke to her.

In Acts 10:9 Peter is described as having a vision while on a rooftop. A little phrase at the beginning of this passage reveals why Peter was able to receive such a powerful communication from God. 'Peter went up on the roof to pray.'

We don't know what Peter was praying for but what we do know is that now more than ever before Peter was learning the secret of being dependent on God. Just before this event he had been used powerfully to minister healing and raise someone from the dead but he did not think, 'I'm there, I've got it!' Instead, he went up on the roof to pray.

Receiving the Gifts Through Spirit Inspired Bible Meditation

In Chapter 3, I talked about how we can learn to hear God through the Bible. In the same way when we are seeking God for words of knowledge, prophecies, gifts of healing, faith or wisdom, we can read the Bible with that conscious sense that a certain verse, phrase or even a whole passage may be something that God wants to say to someone prophetically *now*.

One day I was sitting at the front of an Anglican church prior to the evening's concert. This church had an extremely high ceiling and I thought, you could fit another building up there and this church would still be tall! Suddenly, as I was gazing upwards I seemed to 'see' another floor coming into place. It started at the very front of the building and slowly moved backwards until the whole of the church was covered with a new lower ceiling. As I was wondering what on earth this meant, the thought came to me that I should read Isaiah 58. The middle of this chapter calls God's people to serve those in need, feed the hungry, clothe the naked, help the oppressed. God seemed to be saying that He wanted them to build an extra floor in the church and use it to provide practical help and accommodation for those in need.

This was a very directive prophecy and I was reluctant to share it. After all if they acted on it and it was wrong it could cost them thousands! After I prayed, however, I still had a deep sense of peace that I should share it.

At the end of the concert I was amazed to hear that God had recently spoken to them in exactly the same way and led them to the same verses! They had actually begun to make enquiries to see how feasible it would be to have another floor put in and in doing so had discovered that the church was no longer structurally sound. A new church was going to be built and just at the time I brought that prophecy, they had been praying for confirmation as to whether they should have extra space included in the plan to accommodate the needy!

In that situation I had a vision first but on its own it did not mean anything. It was when I turned to the verses that the meaning of the extra floor in the vision became clear. As I read the passage it seemed that each word took on a '*now*' significance, that this was what God was saying *now* to this particular fellowship, that this was to be their goal and emphasis from then on.

Jesus Himself was fully entrenched in the Scriptures before He entered into His ministry. As He taught, often in the midst of violent opposition and hatred, He would point to different Scriptures, saying, 'This is to fulfil . . .'

The most memorable occasion was when He read out Isaiah 61:1–4 'The Spirit of the Sovereign Lord is on me, because the Lord has anointed me to preach good news to the poor' and then said to them, 'Today this scripture is fulfilled in your hearing' (Luke 4:21).

Jesus is the fulfilment of Scripture. John describes Him as 'The Word' and now that Jesus, through His Holy Spirit, has come to live with us, the Word of God has become a living, present fulfilment in our lives. It is a bit like when we go to do a concert for a church. Before we go, we send them Marilyn's publicity material including photos and a short written biography. Often, members of the church have heard Marilyn's tapes and been blessed which has then led to them asking Marilyn to come and sing in person. When the concert takes place Marilyn tells her story, but it is no longer just a dry account on a sheet of paper but living words, living emotions, real present struggles and victories. Again, when she sings, it is the same songs that are on the tapes but instead of something that's been recorded five years before, it is her living voice singing from her heart songs that she believes God is telling her to sing there and then to speak to people in the audience.

Listening Through our Eyes

One day I was in a concert with Marilyn. I was quietly praying for the Holy Spirit to come on the audience. There was a beautiful flower display just beyond her and I admired the harmony of delicate colours and shapes.

I noticed that although the display as a whole looked fresh and full of life, there were some flowers that were beginning to wilt and one or two were even dead. This was normal, but suddenly I couldn't seem to stop thinking about it. It was as if it was taking on a significance and an urgency that went beyond mere flowers. Silently I began to pray and asked God if He was trying to tell me something through these flowers. I then had the thought to look in 1 Peter 1:24–5. I had no idea what this would say and was startled to read 'All men are like grass, and all their glory is like the flowers of the field; the grass withers and the flowers fall, but the word of the Lord stands for ever.'

I wondered if this might be a general word for everyone but as I continued to pray the thought came into my mind that it was for an individual there. Someone who had repeatedly resisted God and had gone high up the achievement ladder. God seemed to say, 'He is trusting in his achievements and power and so far they have served him well, but he is too proud to admit his need of me and has repeatedly rejected my word. Therefore just like those flowers wilt and die even in the midst of their beauty, so in his work and in his life he will crumble and die, even in the midst of all he has achieved, unless he humbles himself and accepts my word.'

'But Lord,' I said, 'I can't say he will die, that's awful!'

But I couldn't get away from this thought. The more I tried to diminish it or get out of saying it at all, the greater the sense of urgency. My mouth was dry and my heart pounding when at last I got up to speak. As soon as I began, the fear lifted and the words came with an authority and conviction that astonished me. Even as I spoke I became aware that behind the stern words was an overflow of yearning love for this man. The realisation brought tears to my eyes as I sensed the anguish in God's heart and His longing to be able to love him. I believe that although I only spoke the words God had given me, this underlying love was expressed too.

A man later approached one of the church counsellors for prayer. It turned out that he was one of the most influential business men in the town and was a committed atheist. He began to weep as he described how when the word was spoken something within him seemed to break and for the first time he saw what he was really like. That night he reached out for God's forgiveness and found a new goal for living, Jesus.

This word/prophecy came as I was glancing at a very ordinary thing, a flower display. I was not expecting a word but God still broke into my consciousness with the realisation that somehow the display was significant. I could easily at that stage have ignored this feeling thinking it was my imagination, instead I talked to God about it. That was the first stage but it needed more than that! If you read the previous chapter you will have noticed that when I contemplate God through His creation I expect Him to say nice things! My natural reaction would be to think something like, 'If God had made each flower so full of fragrance and colour how much more has He made us to be beautiful . . .'

If I had said something like that some people may have been encouraged, but its real object would have just carried on the same as before! That was probably why God also led me to the scripture, because it broke into my set way of thinking and predisposed me to hearing what He really wanted me to say.

An Ecstatic Experience?

Often when people think of hearing God through dreams, visions and pictures, they feel it must be some kind of overwhelming, ecstatic experience where their minds and imaginations are taken out of their control, rather like having a hallucination. Of course this may happen sometimes and there are testimonies of this type of experience. I believe, however, that on many occasions, God wants to speak powerfully through things that are completely ordinary, like that flower display.

When God first called Jeremiah He said to him '"What do you see, Jeremiah?" "I see the branch of an almond tree," I replied' (Jer. 1:11).

God told Jeremiah he had seen correctly. At that stage there was no spiritual revelation about the branch and it may have been that Jeremiah was looking at an actual, present, almond tree when God asked him what he could see. The point is, God was teaching Jeremiah to 'see' in a specific way, to focus on the one thing, rather than on the whole scene, to be prepared for something ordinary and commonplace to be the carrier of a prophetic message. After this God asked Jeremiah again what he could see and this time Jeremiah had a definite vision. '"I see a boiling pot, tilting away from the north," I answered' (Jer. 1:13).

Jeremiah would have been used to seeing a boiling pot, just the same as we would be used to seeing a saucepan! But now, instead of just seeing something that was a normal part of everyday life, he saw with his spiritual eyes that this particular pot was doing something strange. It was 'tilting away from the north'. Obviously, if a real boiling pot was to tilt over, disaster would follow, the contents would be spilt and lost and people could be burnt. Maybe thoughts of these natural consequences were going through Jeremiah's mind when God broke in again and began to reveal in specific words, the awful and awesome things that were about to take place when the 'boiling pot' of God's judgment was released against Jerusalem. The rest of the book of Jeremiah is full of specifically pronounced words and prophecies rather than visions, but it is the initial vision through something concrete and ordinary that opens Jeremiah's ears to hearing the deep truths of God.

I've watched how on a film the camera suddenly homes in on something. One minute people will be chatting in a room, the next all you can see is a close up of a car pulling in to a darkened drive. The music plays eerily in the background and then it switches back to the people again who seem completely unaware of anything wrong. A few minutes later the car is shown again and you know that soon something is going to happen. The music gets more dramatic and if you're anything like me you'll be sitting on the edge of your chair willing the people to realise before it's too late!

This 'homing in' to ordinary things is what gives the film its suspense. I believe that God uses the same technique by making us home in on something seemingly ordinary that then becomes significant. In the film, especially if it is a thriller, I find that my heart starts pounding and my hands go clammy as I anticipate what is about to happen. In the same way, I and many others can experience physical symptoms when God reveals something supernaturally.

God's Still Small Voice

As I have grown more experienced in recognising the Lord's voice I have realised that God never bowls us over when He wants to speak to us but whispers to us in a 'still, small voice'. When I was at senior school I had a headmistress who always spoke like a sergeant-major. Even if it was just you and her in the room she would still shout. Many of us feel that God will be like this, and maybe even want Him to be. After all, in some ways it's safer to be able to say, 'God overwhelmed me, God forced me . . .'

But God wants us to be working in partnership with Him, obeying Him because we want to and because we have a holy fear and reverence for Him, not because we fear Him as a tyrant. That is why He has given us His Holy Spirit so that we may come to hear His words to us in our own minds.

'The Spirit searches all things, even the deep things of God . . . We have not received the spirit of the world but the Spirit who is from God, that we may understand what God has freely given us . . . "For who has known the mind of the Lord that he may instruct Him?" But we have the mind of Christ' (1 Cor. 2:10–16).

We have the mind of Christ but we also think our own thoughts and that is where the conflict can arise sometimes. Listening to God through the spiritual gifts always means bypassing our own knowledge and understanding, sometimes causing us to say or do things that are directly opposed to what we think. I often feel that the least thing I want to do is share a possible word from God. I feel it will be wrong or that I've misunderstood it. In his book, *The Hot Line*, Peter Lawrence tells how when he first started to get words of knowledge for people in his church, he tried to get out of sharing them, sure that in such a small group of people they couldn't possibly be right. In the end he did share them but in a very vague kind of way saying 'a pain in the back' rather than 'in the spine' for example. Afterwards he had to kick himself when someone came up with a pain in the back which turned out to be a spinal problem![2]

To share what we feel God is saying is a risky business and makes us feel very vulnerable. I was encouraged when reading the Bible to realise that people then also had doubts even though to us they seem like spiritual giants.

Take Ananias for example:

> The Lord told him, 'Go to the house of Judas . . . and ask for a man from Tarsus named Saul . . . In a vision he has seen a man named Ananias come and place his hands on him to restore his sight.'
>
> 'Lord,' Ananias answered, 'I have heard many reports about this man . . . and he has come here . . . to arrest all who call on your name.'
>
> But the Lord said to Ananias, 'Go! This man is my chosen instrument . . .'
>
> Then Ananias went . . . (Acts 9:11–17)

No Need to Compare Ourselves

Many of us feel 'if only I could hear God like "so and so" then I'd know I was doing OK!'

I am always thinking this. I have sometimes been in churches where people have given long powerful prophecies full of the authority of God and I have looked at my own efforts and thought, 'Mine are no good because they're not like that.'

The thing I am growing to realise is that our God is a God who loves variety and has poured this extravagant love out into His creation. If you think of the millions of types of wild flowers on an ordinary hillside or the fact that every snowflake or every fingerprint is different, you will begin to get a glimpse of what I mean. Because we alone out of all creation are made in the image of God, then it is a foregone conclusion that this variety and uniqueness will be part of our characters. God *will* speak to us differently, both because we are different and because God is too! If we use different ways to speak to our colleagues, our bosses, our husbands and wives or our children, how much more will God use different ways to speak to us!

I personally tend to hear God more through pictures and visions but Marilyn does more rarely, probably because as she is blind, pictures are not a natural medium for her. She will often have prophetic words or words of knowledge but when she does have a picture it is all the more powerful because God has shown her something that humanly she could not imagine. Marilyn can often 'see' the heart of a person where outward appearances seem to say exactly the opposite. Recently a lady came up to us. She was all smiles as she said she just wanted some more of the Lord's blessing. I started to pray along those lines and at the end, the lady, eyes closed, was still smiling. Marilyn then said, 'I've got this sense you've been very dominated by your mother.' The lady absolutely burst into tears, fell forward onto Marilyn's lap and sobbed for the next half hour! If Marilyn had been trying to copy me, this lady would have probably gone away with her grief still bottled up, but because Marilyn trusted God she was deeply touched.

The prophets of the Old Testament all heard God in unique

ways. For many, it was a case of 'The word of the Lord' came to . . . and then they would speak out prophetically what they had heard. Ezekiel, Daniel and John, in the New Testament, all had visions that were beyond the reaches of their experience or imagination. Hosea, and also Ezekiel, both felt compelled to perform strange actions which became prophetic signs to the nation. God opened the mouth of a donkey to speak to Balaam, spoke to Moses through a burning bush and came to Abraham as a man. Jonah rebelled against God and was swallowed by a fish for three days. This became, generations later, a prophetic symbol of Jesus' death but at the time Jonah heard God through specific words being given to him.

Knowing God and Perceiving what He Wants to Say

I always find the story of Jonah fascinating. He was so like us in many ways. When God spoke to him and told him to go to Nineveh to preach against their sin and declare the Lord's judgment, he ran away! The reason he ran away was because he was afraid the Lord would not show up and fulfil the word! 'What will they think of me then?' kept running through his mind. It is so easy to have our thoughts on what people will think of us rather than seeking the Lord to know what He is really saying behind the bare bones of the message. Even when Jonah eventually preached the word to Nineveh he still hadn't cottoned on to what God really wanted to do.

> The Ninevites believed God. They declared a fast and all of them, from the greatest to the least, put on sackcloth . . . When God saw what they did and how they turned from their evil ways, He had compassion and did not bring upon them the destruction He had threatened. But Jonah was greatly displeased and became angry. (Jonah 3:5–4:1)

Jonah wanted God to carry out His threat of destruction because it would confirm him in his role and make him believable but he forgot that the heart of God is always to forgive rather than judge. I have often been in churches where prophecies or words have been given exposing things like sexual sin or bad habits. Sometimes, when people have responded they have been lambasted with judging words instead of given the chance to respond to the Lord's forgiveness. Marilyn once prayed with a young man in this position. He had been struggling for years against homosexual tendencies and several times had publicly repented when a relevant word was given in his church. Each time, however, the people praying with him had focused on the awful nature of his sin making him feel so afraid and condemned that he became completely withdrawn. He was talking with Marilyn about something else but she kept getting the word 'homosexual' come to her mind. Eventually she asked him very gently if he had any problems of that nature. When he responded she continued seeking the Lord and a long buried emotional hurt to do with his mother was revealed. At the end, although he still had a lot to work through, he knew that the Lord had met with him and loved him and was giving him the power to change.

I feel it is vitally important that we make the Bible our priority foundation for all other experiential forms of listening to God. The more we listen to what it reveals to us of God's character and purposes and what we should or should not be expecting to happen, the more likely we will be to have words of knowledge, prophecies, visions and dreams that are in line with the truth. Not just the truth of facts, but the truth of God's character. The gifts are just tools drawing us, and those with whom we share them, close to our Father's heart.

Dreams – Are they God's Messengers?

Carol, a friend of ours, sent us a transcript of a beautiful dream that God gave her one night. Carol is serving a life sentence and despite having become a Christian in prison was still unable to forgive herself and let go of her past. On this particular day she felt desperate for some quiet, but the endless prison noises hounded her. In the end she fell asleep as she sat on her bed, and began to dream.

In the dream she was on a mountain top in a violent storm. As she cried out to God to help her she saw a light in a hut. She was about to enter when she realised someone was inside and as she gazed became aware that it was Jesus. She turned away knowing she could not possibly be with Him.

To quote her own words:

> I heard a voice so full of love say, 'Carol, come in out of the rain, can't you see the door is open?' I turned back and all the fear disappeared as He smiled just for me and beckoned me in. Inside it was so calm and peaceful, nothing but the gentle crackling of logs on the fire. I couldn't look at Him but I sat in front of the fire and just kept my eyes to the floor. 'Look at me, Carol,' He said. Then I lifted my head and looked into His eyes. They searched the deepest corners of my heart, they could see everything I had ever done and also the very thing I had been asking Him to forgive. I found they were not only searching, but shining, not because my sins did not matter but shining with compassion that went beyond what I had done and saw the desire I had to serve Him.

The storm over, Jesus accompanied Carol down the mountain then turned back. At first Carol was devastated at the thought of losing Him then came to the realisation that:

I can never really be parted from Him. Something wonderful has happened . . . He is right here inside of me. It is as though my heart is that building and I have gained Him forever. There are no words to describe how I feel. I am not just me any more. I am free. I feel so full of joy, all I want is to show everyone my love for Jesus. Inside my heart is a peace I have never had and a strength that can push away the worst storm. Nothing can destroy them.

On waking and returning to the reality of prison life, Carol wrote: 'Just a dream maybe it was but not the Presence that is so real still here as I write.'

Marilyn and I both wept as we read this. We had been corresponding with Carol for a long time trying to show her that she was forgiven. But God knew, in His mercy, that Carol needed more than words. This dream, full of such powerful pictorial images of the love of Jesus, destroyed the tormenting images of her past and released her to know the joy of her forgiveness.

Dreams and visions are similar in that they are moving pictures expressing truths about our lives or the things of God or something that is about to happen. The difference between them is that we have a vision when we are awake and conscious, but when we have a dream we are asleep. I used to feel that because we are asleep it would be impossible to know if it is from God, or just a normal dream, or even from the devil?

Although I am not very experienced in this area I have come to believe that, even though in many ways dreams are out of our control, there are things we can do to help influence our dreams for the good. I remember once, I was about to go to bed at the end of a tiring day. I had had a bad argument with a friend that afternoon and as I went to sleep I was still going over and over what had happened. Suddenly a thought seemed to break into the turmoil: 'Don't go to sleep angry because it will affect your dreams and make you vulnerable to the evil one. You will wake up heavy and tired but if you forgive your friend and allow me to forgive you then you will go to sleep at peace, your dreams will be blessed and you will wake up refreshed.'

I was amazed by this thought and suddenly realised that it tallied with the verse in Ephesians, 'Do not let the sun go down while you are still angry' (Eph. 4:26).

I asked God to forgive me and handed over to Him everything that had happened. I did sleep well that night and although my dreams weren't anything out of the ordinary, neither were they oppressive and distressing like they usually were after a difficult day. When I woke up I felt refreshed and much more on top spiritually.

I told Marilyn and she too began to notice a difference in her quality of sleep. Since that time I have experienced more dreams that I believe have come from God and have had more of a clear sense when the devil has been trying to attack me through a dream. I have also found that there are many passages in the Psalms that refer to God watching over us as we sleep and I now try to consciously thank the Lord for that and rest anything that is worrying me in His hands before I go to sleep.

Knowing our Motives

When I had been with Marilyn about three months, I was just growing used to my 'role' as the team's prophet when Carol Joyce joined the team as Marilyn's secretary and road manager. For a while all was fine. I really liked Carol and admired her administrative and practical gifts. Then one day she had a vision in an evangelistic crusade. It was very powerful and led to several becoming Christians. I was thrilled about that but felt a bit thrown too. Surely it was me who had prophecies? But I hadn't had any yet this crusade. Was I losing my role? Over the next few weeks Carol often had thoughts and ideas for the concerts while I had less and less. In desperation I thought, 'I *will* have a word!' I gave a long, involved 'prophecy' in the concert that night and sat down satisfied, I'd done it!

Later I read a few verses as usual before going to sleep. I was tired and hurried with my reading. Suddenly a verse caught my attention: 'I consider everything a loss compared to the surpassing greatness of knowing Christ Jesus my Lord' (Phil. 3:8).

It was as if a light was shining on my heart. I began to sob as I realised what I'd been doing. 'O Lord,' I whispered, 'I've been so concerned about me, so wanting to hold onto my role, so resentful about Carol. Lord, I've pushed you out, I've forgotten that "surpassing greatness of knowing you". Lord, it's not even my role, it's just things you've given me! Please forgive me, Lord.'

I gave the Lord back my prophetic gifts that night and felt that was an end to them. That did not matter any more, the important thing was for the Lord to have centre place again. For a few concerts I had nothing and Carol continued to share her thoughts, but now I felt at peace about it. To my surprise, about a fortnight later I started to get that old inner awareness that God wanted to speak and that night He gave me several words that were all responded to. As soon as I recognised the Giver and gave Him the glory rather than 'my' gifts, He released me to hear Him again. It made me echo Paul's words:

> Oh, the depth of the riches of the wisdom and knowledge of God! How unsearchable His judgments, and His paths beyond tracing out! 'Who has known the mind of the Lord? Or who has been His counsellor? Who has ever given to God, that God should repay him? For from Him and through Him and to Him are all things. To Him be the glory for ever! (Rom. 11:33–6).

The Way of Jesus

Jesus never did healings, deliverances, or miracles, prophesied or had words of knowledge just for their own sake, as a demonstration of His power. In fact, when some people wanted Him to do that very thing He was very angry with them and refused! Jesus always did these things to meet needs. Jesus loved people and His heart was broken by the needs He saw. He wept even when He knew He was going to perform an outstanding miracle. He cared and because He cared, He acted. He still cares and He still acts today, through me and you. That is why He has given us the Holy Spirit. The gifts are not for us to prove how spiritual we are but are tools to enable us to meet people's needs and to bring in the kingdom of God 'on earth as it is in heaven' effectively. 'But you will receive power when the Holy Spirit comes on you; and you will be my witnesses . . . to the ends of the earth' (Acts 1:8).

Stepping out in Faith

It says in Hebrews that 'without faith it is impossible to please God' (Heb. 11:6). To follow up what we hope is a divinely-inspired hunch, always requires a big step of faith. I often feel 'but I can't share that! I can't understand what it means! I'm sure I should be saying this not that . . .' I forget that it gives joy to God when we step out in faith even if we make mistakes!

In his book *How To Live Like A King's Kid* Harold Hill tells how God gave him an extremely practical word of knowledge one day. His company supplied complex electrical equipment to a power station and Hill was in charge of the final checking before handing it over. On this particular day Hill had a phone call to say that the equipment would not work despite having two groups of highly qualified technicians working on it for four days. Not knowing what to do, Hill prayed and a picture came to his mind of what was wrong.

When he arrived he went straight to the part he had seen in the picture and told the technician what to do. The technician's scornful manner confirmed his own feeling of being ridiculous but he pressed on. The technician obeyed the simple instructions and in moments the equipment was working![3]

There have been numerous times when I definitely have got it wrong. Just the other week I was taking part in a concert and while sitting on the stage became aware of a young girl in the third row. I wondered if there was anything God wanted to say to her and the thought came to my mind that she had had an abortion.

That is always a sensitive area so I prayed that the Lord would confirm it. When she voluntarily asked for prayer later, that seemed to be the confirmation I needed so as a suitable moment arrived I asked her. The answer was a definite no! I apologised and we prayed about the real issues but I felt very sad that I'd 'heard' God wrongly.

The problem is, when we make a mistake we often feel guilty and lose our confidence. That makes us draw back from God and instead of receiving His forgiveness we think we will not be trusted with a word again. God does not say the same and as Isaiah learnt, we need not draw back.

> The Sovereign Lord has given me an anointed tongue, to know the word that sustains the weary. He wakens me morning by morning, wakens my ear to listen like one being taught. The Sovereign Lord has opened my ears, and I have not been rebellious; I have not drawn back. (Isa. 50:4–5)

On another occasion a lady came to Marilyn and me for prayer at the end of a concert. She was having problems with a relationship and after talking a while, but not really coming to any clear solution, we began to pray together. Marilyn invited the Holy Spirit to come and I silently asked Him if there was any root cause for her problems. The thought grew in my heart that she had had an abortion that she had never forgiven herself for. Abortions again! I prayed the Lord would give me a real sense of peace if He wanted me to share this thought and He did. Very hesitantly I asked her if there was anything she'd ever done that she really regretted. The answer was 'lots of things!' so I knew I needed to be specific. 'Have you ever had an abortion?' I asked gently. She burst into tears and sobbed violently. It turned out she'd had it fifteen years before but the memory and pain were still raw. Through the next half hour God led us as to how to pray for this dear lady. It was different to how we'd prayed for anyone else with the same problem but at the end she'd not only received God's forgiveness and forgiven herself but also seen a vision of her baby held safely in God's arms. She left that meeting at peace, a transformed woman.

The Most Important Thing

In this chapter I have tried to express some of the things I have been learning over the years about hearing God through His gifts. I am still very much a beginner and I know that there are many Christians that are far more knowledgeable and experienced than me. I have therefore not tried to analyse or set out in order what each gift is but at the end of this chapter is a list of books which do and which I personally recommend.

Some of you may feel confused at the way I have skipped around from words to prophecies to visions and then back again, but I felt that for me, the important things are the underlying factors that are common to them all. That God, as our 'Daddy', wants to give all of us these gifts and that they are given to us 'for the common good'. To enable us to reach out in the power and love of God to the needy people around us, to proclaim God's kingdom, and to build up the living Church of God.

In other chapters I will be discussing the gifts again in relation to how we can converse with God, how we can use visions in our prayer life, how we can learn to recognise the signs of the times. All these things overlap which is why I've looked at how we can actually begin to receive revelations and sort out our motives rather than analysing the gifts individually.

The gifts of God are wonderful, exciting and crucial to us truly being effective as Christians but we must always remember that the most important thing for us is to be full of the love of Christ. The gifts are love's servants!

> 'If I speak in the tongues of men and of angels, but have not love, I am only a resounding gong or a clanging cymbal. If I have the gift of prophecy and can fathom all mysteries and all knowledge, and if I have a faith that can move mountains, but have not love, I am nothing . . . Love never fails. But where there are prophecies, they will cease; where there are tongues, they will be stilled; where there is knowledge, it will pass away . . . the greatest of these is love. (1 Cor. 13:1–2, 8, 13)

OVER TO YOU

1 Read through the list of gifts in 1 Corinthians 12:7 and Joel 2:28. Thank the Lord for any that you have already experienced. Remember that with the exception of speaking in tongues, and even that, if it is shared in a communal setting, all the gifts are to enable us to minister the love of God to others.
2 Ask the Lord for any particular gift you feel you need.

Remember He loves to give, so thank Him He has heard you and in faith receive your gift.

3 Ask the Lord if there is any person or any situation that He wants you to be praying for. Thank Him that He has given you the mind of Christ and ask the Holy Spirit to come and fill you and reveal God's thoughts to you as you pray.

4 In a three-fold action, a) keep your mind and heart focusing on the love of God, b) lift up to Him, for example, the person/situation/coming church meeting that you are praying for and c) either meditatively read a Bible passage, or look with spiritual eyes at the things around you, or listen with spiritual ears for any 'words' or feelings that come to you.

You may feel this is impossible but it is something we do naturally all the time! When you cook you may be keeping an eye on the pan boiling on the hob, while at the same time preparing the fruit for the pudding and planning how to set the table. Or you may meet a friend in the high street and start chatting about your kids while at the same time be writing a mental shopping list and planning what to give your sister for tea! Our minds are able to focus on many things at the same time and if we give this natural gift to God then with practice and the inspiration of the Holy Spirit, we will be able to pray, meditate, 'drift' and hear God all at the same time.

5 If anything comes to your mind ask God to give you a deep sense of peace and an 'inner knowing' if it is from Him, or to distract you and give you a sense of uneasiness if it is not from Him. If you think it is something you need to share with others, ask Him for a gift of wisdom to know how, and when, to share

6 When you do share it ask the Lord to cover your words and manner with His love. Speak sensitively – sometimes I've given words and left no room for people to escape. I'm learning not to say 'Thus saith the Lord' or 'God says do this

do that . . .' but something like 'I think the Lord may be saying . . . but don't worry if it doesn't witness with you.'

7 Go for it! If God has entrusted us with something precious we need to obey Him and share it. Don't worry about making a mistake, I make them all the time and so does everyone! God is full of mercy and if He was worried about our mistakes He would never have given us His gifts!

Reading on Gifts

Dennis and Rita Bennett, *The Holy Spirit and You* (Kingsway, 1971).
David Pytches, *Come Holy Spirit* (Hodder & Stoughton, 1985).
Peter H. Lawrence, *The Hot Line* (Kingsway, 1990).
Joyce Huggett, *Listening To God* (Hodder & Stoughton, 1986).
Clifford Hill, *Prophecy Past and Present* (Highland Books, 1989).

6
Conversing with God

A Dialogue with God

One night we were travelling home after a concert. I was very tired but couldn't seem to relax. The other team members were all leaving in a few weeks and as yet we hadn't found anyone to replace them. We had been experiencing some financial difficulties too and that night I couldn't seem to stop worrying.

'Oh, Lord, please work it all out,' I prayed, shifting round in my seat.

Suddenly some words seemed to break into my restless thoughts.

> 'When you drive home like this, you don't worry or fret about how you're going to get back, you just get into your part of the van and do your own thing, more often than not you go to sleep! Without any effort of will you trust the boys to drive you home. Even if something were to go wrong you'd still trust that they'd be able to sort it out. Why don't you trust me in the same way?'

I was startled. Was I dreaming? But no, I knew I was wide awake. The words had come with such vivid clarity that I realised it must be God speaking to me. I could sense His gentle rebuke in that last question and felt I had to respond, and so began an incredible conversation with God.

Me: 'But getting home isn't a problem so there's no cause for me to worry.'

God: 'But you could be worrying, you could be sitting upright in your chair, watching as the van approaches every roundabout or junction. You could be agonising over each stage of driving and even be nagging Alistair and Nick to do the things that make up driving.

Me: 'But that's silly because they're drivers and I'm not so there's no need for me to worry like that. They're experts!'

God: 'But if they are expert at driving how much more am I expert at seeing you through difficulties? I am Almighty, so if you can trust in their learnt skills to the extent that you can sleep throughout a dangerous journey, how much more should you be able to trust and relax in me? In my expertise, my power, my promises, my omniscience, my integrity, my faithfulness and my love? At the moment you are at the stage of forcing yourself to trust me. In other words, sitting on the edge of your chair and agonising over the driver's moves. But I want to bring you to that point where your heart instinctively trusts me and where you can completely rest in me.'

This experience in the van proved to be a milestone one for me. I had, by now, experienced hearing the Lord through things like words of knowledge, and the Bible and the natural world, but to hear the Lord in a conversational way seemed an altogether different kettle of fish. Yet this had seemed such a natural thing, just as if I was talking with Marilyn or another friend. The thoughts that came to my mind in response to my questions were definite and strong, both challenging and changing the way I was thinking myself, yet at the same time it was almost as if they were my own thoughts. I was amazed by the wisdom and humour inherent in them and realised that God had spoken to me just as a dad might talk to his child.

Rest in my Love

Marilyn was travelling on her own one day and began to panic when she was waiting for a bus. It was a busy road with cars roaring past all the time making it hard to hear, and when her bus was due several came at once. Eventually someone helped her on but Marilyn still felt very tense and anxious.

Suddenly, the Lord seemed to say to her: 'Why don't you just relax and enjoy the journey? I have got you here safely, I am in charge of every stage of this journey. You could have made it a lot easier for yourself if you hadn't got into such a flap! Just rest in me for I am with you.'

Marilyn was amazed by this. She knew it was the Lord and asked Him to forgive her for not trusting Him. As she continued listening to Him she felt her anxiety melting away. She drank in His peace and love and it seemed almost as if His words were taking shape like a song that He was singing to her.

Rest in my love, relax in my care
and know that my presence will always be there.
You are my child, and I care for you,
There's nothing my love and my power cannot do.

To Marilyn's amazement, she later found that these words fitted exactly into a piece of music she had composed a short time before. When the music had come to her mind she had loved the tune and the feeling behind it, but she couldn't think of any lyrics to fit it. These words were perfectly right.

Since 'Rest in my Love' has been recorded people have written countless letters to say how much it has helped them to trust in God and rest their anxieties in Him. As Marilyn talked to God and then heard His loving answer, it became a conversation that not only blessed her but many others too.

On both these occasions God chose to break into our thoughts in a specific way, stopping our negative fretting in its tracks, throwing light on the situation and challenging us to turn in a whole new direction.

God's Longing to be Intimate

I am always moved when I read the opening verses of Hosea 11. They express God's longing to be close to us and His grief that even though He has done everything to draw us into a deep relationship, we have refused His love.

> When Israel was a child, I loved him, and out of Egypt I called my son. But the more I called Israel, the further they went from me. They sacrificed to the Baals and they burned incense to images. It was I who taught Ephraim to walk, taking them by the arms; but they did not realise it was I who healed them. I led them with cords of human kindness, with ties of love; I lifted the yoke from their neck and bent down to feed them (Hos. 11:1–4).

Even though the nation Israel was so selfish and rebellious, God still called them His son. He loved them as a father and wanted to express that love to them daily in an intimate, give-and-take relationship.

I believe that before we can even contemplate coming to God in prayer, we need to affirm the truth in our own hearts that we are not about to talk to a remote and distant God, but 'Our Father who art in heaven'. The One who calls us His 'beloved' children and loves to speak to us. 'For you did not receive a spirit that makes you a slave again to fear, but you received the Spirit of sonship. And by Him we cry, "Abba, Father". The Spirit himself testifies with our spirit that we are God's children' (Rom. 8:15–16).

He Wants to Talk with us

When God spoke to me the first time, I remember feeling awed and amazed. It was not just that He spoke with such loving compassion. It was the fact that He also listened to me and then responded again, just as in a normal conversation. It was as if He actually wanted to hear what I had to say, even though my words were full of self pity and anger. It makes me blush with shame to think that while He, the source of all our wisdom and knowledge, the One who has promised to be our counsellor and has given us the very mind of Christ, chose to listen so lovingly to me, I was so often blind to my need to listen to Him.

Is our Prayer Like a One-Way Phone Call?

Marilyn often tells of how a friend of hers rang up one day. She seemed to have a lot to talk about and Marilyn just could not get a word in edgeways! In the end this friend talked non-stop for two hours and Marilyn felt so bored that she even went and put the kettle on for a cup of tea! When she came back to the phone her friend hadn't even noticed! I always laugh when I hear this and think, 'How could anyone hold a conversation like that?', yet it is in just that way that we so often talk with God.

In the Bible, although there are several examples of people praying to God in this monologue kind of way, there is a definite difference in that the prayers stem from a deep anguish of heart that needed expressing, rather than people just bringing God a shopping list of needs like we so often do today. Always there is a deep conviction that even though God might not be answering verbally, He is listening and responding.

'I will Come in and Eat with Him'

One day Marilyn had a Dutch friend come for dinner. On the phone before she came Marilyn asked her what she would like for pudding. 'Jelly please!' was the response. 'We never have that in Holland.'

Good, Marilyn thought, that will be nice and easy! She knew English cooking doesn't always have a very good reputation so she was pleased when the beef bourgignon seemed to be doing so well. Just before her friend arrived she checked the jelly only to find to her dismay that it was still runny! Just then the doorbell rang and in a panic she thrust it into the freezer!

Dinner-time came, her friend was loving the meal and just as they were scraping the last bits up, she said, 'I'm so looking forward to my jelly!'

Marilyn's heart sank, she'd totally forgotten it. Jumping up with a muttered 'hold on' she rushed out to the freezer. As she had feared, the jelly was a solid block of ice!

Standing there with it in her hands, she sent up a frantic prayer for help. She wasn't sure what the Lord could do about it, but she certainly had no idea herself! Suddenly a thought came into her mind so vividly it was like someone speaking next to her.

'Put it in the microwave!'

Marilyn was so startled she nearly dropped the jelly! She had only purchased the microwave two days before and hadn't used it yet. She would never have thought of putting it in there! This must be you, Lord, she thought, as she gingerly opened the door. 'Well, how long do I cook a frozen jelly for?'

When it came out the jelly was sort of set with little frosty bits in! Her friend said she absolutely loved it!

In Revelation 3, Jesus makes His impassioned appeal to us all: 'Here I am! I stand at the door and knock. If anyone hears my voice and opens the door, I will come in and eat with him, and he with me' (Rev. 3:20).

When I read this verse, I was amazed at the intimate picture it conveyed. Marilyn and I, and the rest of our team, do a lot of eating with people because we are always staying in different people's houses. Sometimes our hosts are a bit shy and self conscious when we first arrive and the conversation around the table can be rather stiff and polite. Once they relax though, and realise that even though Marilyn is a singer, she is a completely ordinary and down-to-earth woman, the conversation begins to flow and over the meal we may share stories and they tell us about their own lives.

Jesus says, 'If only you will open the door I will come in and we can share a meal together'. The Gospels all tell of how Jesus loved to spend time with people in their homes. Even people whom the religious leaders spurned because of their sinful lives, Jesus took pleasure in visiting. He didn't care that by doing this He was throwing His own reputation in jeopardy, He just wanted to be with people, talking with them and sharing their lives. As people loosened up and the talk began to flow, Jesus would tell stories, respond to people's questions and even their unspoken thoughts. His answers would often probe deeply into people's motives and attitudes and as they listened they were changed.

Jesus is making the same appeal to us now. He says that our lives are His dwelling place and He is calling to us to open the door and share them with Him. He is calling all the time but it is as we choose to hear His voice and respond that the way will be opened for Jesus to come in.

Hearing God's Wisdom will make us Grow in Faith

We often feel that we need to have the answer to every problem and if we don't know what to do we panic. But God says He is our wisdom and as we come to Him and ask Him He will give us wisdom generously, without finding fault. He says in Isaiah '"For my thoughts are not your thoughts, nor are my ways your ways . . . as the heavens are higher than the earth, so are my ways higher than your ways and my thoughts than your thoughts"' (Isa. 55:8–9).

Once, during the time when Marilyn was teaching, she was peeling some potatoes before she left for work. She wasn't sure if she had enough time to finish them but couldn't feel her Braille watch to check the time because she had wet hands. So she said to the Lord, 'Have I got time to finish these 'taters before I need to go, Lord?'

As she prayed the answer 'yes' seemed to come to her mind, so she confidently finished the potatoes before looking at her watch. To her horror, she only had five minutes to get there but it was a ten minute walk! She flung her instruments into the rucksack, put the harness on her guide-dog and shot off down the road.

Suddenly the thought came to her mind, 'There is no need for you to run, you can walk sedately if you want to, you've got plenty of time.'

'I can't have,' thought Marilyn, puzzled, but she was sure it was the Lord so she slowed right down and walked sedately to the bus stop. When she got there no one else was waiting so as soon as she heard someone passing by she asked them if the W4 had gone.

'Yes dear, it went five minutes ago,' was the answer.

'Blow it,' Marilyn scolded herself, 'You must be mad, you think you're hearing the Lord but you've just got your head in the clouds. Now you've missed the bus!' But as she fumed she still felt sure that it was the Lord's voice she had heard, so she prayed, 'Well, Lord, you told me to slow down and now I've missed the bus, but you'll just have to get me to school now as I've only got three minutes!'

Just as she finished praying she heard a car come round the corner and draw up next to her tooting its horn. A voice called out to her:

'Hello Marilyn, it's Fred! Where are you going?'

'The Girls' Grammar,' she replied.

'Oh, I'm going that way, jump in!'

Marilyn walked into her classroom just as the bell was ringing!

This situation shows that as her Father, God cared enough for her to want to help her in her daily life but He also wanted to stretch her faith. When Marilyn felt He was telling her to slow down on her way to the bus stop she did so despite the fact that humanly it did not make any sense. When she realised that the bus had gone she still put her faith in the certainty that it was God who had spoken to her and expected Him to do something about her predicament. God did do something, but the upshot of that was not simply that Marilyn got to school in time, but that she had a new faith and expectancy that even if circumstances failed her, God was still in control and would work with power on her behalf in a way that would make her more dependent on Him rather than just on the things around her.

Conversing with God Brings Growth and Change

I sometimes feel that I can't possibly come to God in prayer and expect Him to hear and answer me because of all the wrong things I've done. They feel like an impassable gulf to me and as soon as I start to pray and then try to wait for His answers those things come rushing into my mind and I feel so guilty that I stop praying. This was happening a lot recently, but then, just the other day, God spoke to me in an amazing way in the middle of my church's Sunday morning service.

As soon as the leader said we were going to be quiet for a few minutes and just concentrate on God, all those recent times when I'd avoided praying and reading my Bible rushed into my mind.

'O Lord, forgive me for neglecting you, forgive me for those things I keep doing . . . forgive me, Lord, forgive me . . .' I prayed.

But as usual, I didn't have any real sense that He had forgiven me. I carried on praying desperately, but the worship was just starting up again with me still feeling as dry as ever. Suddenly a little thought seemed to edge itself into my mind.

'As soon as you become aware of something that is wrong you ask me to forgive you, almost as if the words "forgive me" are a magic charm! But you never give yourself time to be truly sorry in your heart for what you have done. I always look at the heart not just the words. Immediately I see that you are sorry and are turning to me in your need, I forgive you. I do not need endless repetitions because I am always waiting with open arms to love and forgive you. All I need is your heart.'

As I 'listened' to these words it was as if I became aware for the first time of how much I had been using God. Tears came to my eyes as I realised how I had been demanding His forgiveness just to make me feel better but still keeping Him at a distance.

'Lord Jesus,' I prayed, 'I've got into such a habit of dealing with my sins in this way, I don't know how to change. Please soften my heart so that I can really be sorry from deep within me.'

As I sat quietly memories began to come to me of times when I had hurt or upset people that were close to me, like Marilyn or the friends I lived with. After each occasion it was the sudden awareness of the hurt and grief I had caused to someone I said I loved that broke me down. God seemed to say to me, 'When you sin you hurt me in that same way. You push me out and wound me.'

In my imagination I saw Jesus in the guise of one of these close friends standing bewildered and hurt by my actions and it was then that my heart really understood and cried out to Him that I was sorry. I couldn't bear to think that I had done such a thing to the One who had done so much for me. This time, even as I was saying how sorry I was, I knew He had forgiven me. It was a peace that filled me from deep inside. I was back, close to Him again, not because of my many repetitions but because I had truly allowed my heart to be sorry before I asked Him to forgive me.

He Knows our Innermost Thoughts, yet Still Loves us

Jesus will never be shocked by us. Sometimes we talk with people in a very superficial way because we are afraid that if we let them see what we are really like they will despise us and reject us. But the Bible shows that He knows all our innermost thoughts and feelings, yet still loves us. This is what Psalm 139 expresses so graphically:

> O Lord, you have examined my heart and know everything about me. You know when I sit or stand. When far away you know my every thought. Every moment you know where I am, you know what I am going to say before I even say it. How precious it is Lord to realise that you are thinking about me constantly . . . (Ps. 139:1–4, 17 [Living Bible])

Rather than retreating in fear, He wants us to talk with Him about those things that are upsetting us and expect to hear His answers, just like when we're sharing our hearts with a close friend.

In her book, *Turning Point*, Jennifer Rees Larcombe tells how God spoke to her one day when she was in a blind rage. Jen had become ill two years before and her health had deteriorated to the point where they knew they could no longer manage to live in the country. Jen was devastated that it had come to this and one day just before they were due to move everything got on top of her. She was in a lot of pain, there were packing cases everywhere and when Tony made an irritating remark it was the last straw, she had to get away! At the bottom of her garden was a large field where cattle grazed. They had passed by her gate that morning and as she tried to negotiate the muddy path on her crutches she slipped and fell face down in a lake of manure. Her legs and arms were too weak for her to get up again so after struggling futilely she was forced to just lie there, trapped by the manure, trapped by her illness and faced by the realisation that there was no one she could blame, except God.

In her own words:

> Lying in the muck I told God what I thought of Him. I was so abusive that I deserved to be struck down by lightning, but instead I really believed He answered me. These words formed themselves inside my head. 'I know about the mess but I want to be in the centre of all those problems with you, and I would be if only you would let me.' As I lay there in all that filth I felt utterly overwhelmed by His love – it really was the most amazing experience of my life . . .[1]

When God responded to the groans and cries of the Israelites who were suffering terribly at the hands of the Egyptians, He took the initiative and revealed Himself to a man called Moses. I often think of Moses as one of the greatest spiritual giants in the Bible and feel that he is so far above anything I could ever attain to, yet at the time God called Moses he was a very weak man. He had been living as a fugitive in a strange land for forty years because of committing murder. Aware of his own sin and many weaknesses, 'Moses hid his face because he was afraid to look at God' (Exod. 3:5).

But these things did not deter God who, throughout the whole amazing conversation, kept assuring Moses of His faithful presence with him and His power and strength to bring about His will. God was not blind to Moses' past but He chose to meet and speak with Moses while the stigma of what he had done was still upon him. Similarly with Paul in the book of Acts, who was actually on his way to bring about imprisonment and death for the Christians when God spoke to him. What I find amazing in all of these instances is the truth that God met them where they were, spoke to them to comfort, heal, challenge and transform them and at the same time led them on, causing them to become at one with His heart and purposes.

Inner Healing and Restoration

Many of us are, deep down, controlled by memories of past failures or hurts. Because God's words are full of transforming power we can be healed as we listen to Him.

'Lord, I am ready to go with you to prison and to death,' Peter said.

But as Jesus knew, this was just another of Peter's impulsive boasts. That night, Peter, overwhelmed by the traumatic events of Jesus' arrest, panicked when he was approached about his identity. When he had stated furiously for the third time that he knew nothing of Jesus, the cock crowed and he suddenly saw Jesus turn and look at him. Faced by the crumbled ashes of his boasts 'he went outside and wept bitterly'(Luke 22:62).

What follows, after Jesus' resurrection, is a most moving biblical example of the way that conversing with God can bring deep growth and inner transformation.

Jesus knew that the depth of grief and remorse Peter was feeling would be paralysing him emotionally and spiritually. He'd already turned away from the ministry God had called him into and tried to go back to his old profession but he'd even failed at that. Jesus knew Peter was sick at heart and would never be able to approach Him himself, so Jesus singled Peter out and asked him simply and quietly, 'Simon, son of John, do you truly love me more than these?'

Peter affirmed his love for Jesus but Jesus knew that was not enough. Peter had denied him three times and could be tortured by that fact for years unless there was some concrete way he could undo what he had done. So Jesus gave Him that opportunity, asking him twice more if he loved Him. Every time Peter answered, Jesus recommissioned him in his ministry. It was a quiet, personal conversation lasting just a couple of minutes but the power of it was such that Peter became a changed man. Gone were the days of idle boasts. He became, as his new name implied, the rock of the disciples and their strongest leader.

Becoming One with God's Heart and Purposes.

In our learning to converse with God we need to move through similar stages as children when they learn to talk. My younger nephew, Michael, is two and at the moment everything he says is to do with something he wants, the egocentric stage! When we are first Christians we are full of what God has done for us and in our prayer life we constantly talk to Him about our problems and needs and hurts, hoping He will help us with them. This is a wonderful and essential aspect of our relationship with our loving Heavenly Father, one that Jesus encouraged us to do again and again. But as in any relationship, we need to move deeper in our conversations with God, to move from that place where we only talk with Him when we want something, to the place where we talk and listen to Him because we want to understand how He feels and thinks. We want to be in tune with Him.

Recently I was attending a listening to God teaching day and during the sharing time a man told us of a mind-blowing thing God had told him one day.

Gerald had had a bad day, he was tired with teaching, and after school his mother, who had Alzheimer's disease, had been very demanding. He'd also visited an old lady later on to give her a hand. As he was returning home he felt very tired but glad that he'd done his bit for the day. He started talking to God, telling Him about his day and half expecting that God would speak some words of love and approval back to him. Hearing nothing of that nature, however, he casually asked God what type of day He'd had. He expected an ordinary, religiousy sort of answer and was already working out in his mind what it would be. He was very startled when suddenly some thoughts started coming into his mind almost as if someone was hesitantly speaking them.

'Well, the same as usual. Hundreds of my daughters have been raped and some murdered too. Thousands of my children killed in futile wars. So many of my smallest children starving and neglected with no hope.'

Gerald was shocked. 'Why did you tell me that Lord, what can I do about it?' he asked.

God said, 'Remember when your daughter was about four, when you had a hard day at work, you'd come home jaded, and then she would come running over to you and hurl herself into your arms. As you loved her and had a cuddle with her, all the world's troubles would fall away – well, all I want is a cuddle, just your companionship and your love.'

Gerald told us that he could hardly believe that God could be telling him this. Could God really want a 'cuddle'? Did He really need Gerald's love and companionship? Those of us in the group were amazed too but later as I was thinking about this, I knew deep down that the answer was yes. Of course, God, just because of who He is, does not have needs in the same way we do. He is already all sufficient! Yet as I prayed and read the Bible it seemed that God was revealing an incredible truth to my heart. That while it was true that He didn't *need* anything from us, He has risked us freely responding to Him out of love rather than force, because He *wants* a true relationship of love with us.

I thought of the time when Jesus, aware of His approaching agony of betrayal and death, asked Peter, James and John to be with Him while He prayed. In that darkest of all moments He longed for those with whom He had spent the last three years to understand what He was about to go through and stand with

Him in it. They failed on that occasion, even though Jesus asked them three times!

When a woman who was a notorious sinner came and poured expensive perfume over Jesus' feet, wiping them with her own hair, Jesus was deeply touched and spoke gently to her, saying that she had done a 'beautiful thing'. Despite her sinful life she had understood what was about to happen to Jesus and was pouring out her love and support in the only way she knew how.

On yet another occasion Jesus wept publicly over Jerusalem, grieving over its hardness of heart and spiritual blindness that was leading to its terrible destruction. Jesus spent many times on His own with His Father in prayer, but on these occasions He showed that He longed for His disciples to think, and feel, and act in harmony with Him.

Jesus said, 'Seek and you will find me.' I am finding in my own life that when I really seek to know Him and understand Him, then step by step He gives me thoughts that draw me closer to His heart and purposes. Just like He did for Abraham.

Abraham was having a rest during the heat of the day when God appeared to him in human form. As I read the story I tried to imagine the scene. I pictured the Lord, hot and dusty from His journey, and Abraham running to get a meal ready. The Lord immediately becoming involved with Abraham's life, eating the meal and chatting about His plans to give them a son.

But it did not end there. As Abraham saw Him off afterwards, the Lord determined to share His heart and plans with him.

'Shall I hide from Abraham what I am about to do?'

There in the roadway the Lord started to express His deep grief over the state of Sodom and Gomorrah. Having met with Abraham on his own ground and talked about the things that were important to him, He now took the conversation to a deeper level, He showed trust in Abraham as a partner who had a right to be 'in the know' and Abraham responded. The ensuing conversation is breathtaking.

> Abraham approached Him and said: 'Will you sweep away the righteous with the wicked? What if there are fifty righteous people in the city? Will you really sweep it away and not spare the place for the sake of the righteous people in it?' . . .
>
> The Lord said, 'If I find fifty righteous people in the city of Sodom I will spare the whole place for their sake.'
>
> Then Abraham spoke up again . . . (Gen. 18:23–7)

While constantly aware of his own nothingness before God, Abraham dared to stand before Him and plead with Him for these doomed towns. He had already seen how real and personal God's love and care was and he now took up that experience of God in his prayer. Running throughout the whole dynamic conversation was the faith born of heart knowledge that his God could not possibly annihilate the righteous together with the wicked. This was no conversation between a master and his servant or even a father and his son. This was God talking with Abraham as if he were an equal, a partner in the future destiny of the world (Gen. 18:1–33).

In the 1970s, a young preacher saw the photograph of a group of young gang-fighters from New York who were standing trial for the murder of a fifteen-year-old polio victim. At first, all David Wilkerson could feel was revulsion. But suddenly, from deep within him, he began to feel a deep grief and anguish. To his shock he realised that he was grieving, not for the victim, but for the murderers! Somehow, as he looked in their eyes, he could sense how lost they were. Puzzled and bewildered by these feelings that seemed so contrary to what he should feel, he began to talk to the Lord about them. It was then that the thought came to his mind: 'I want you to take my love to these boys.' The incredible story of what happened next is recorded in his own book *The Cross and the Switchblade*, and Nicky Cruz's book, *Run Baby Run*.

As I thought about these stories and remembered those times when God had revealed His heart to me I began to perceive the incredible nature of the relationship God had brought me into. The God whom I was beginning to learn to talk to about my daily needs and problems was the same God who was watching over each person, working out His purposes in their lives, in the destiny of towns, nations and the world, and He was calling me to be a part of that with Him.

I remembered Jesus' prayer that all believers 'may be one, Father, just as you are in me and I am in you. May they also be in us so that the world may believe that you have sent me' (John 17:21).

From deep within me I prayed that He would teach me how to talk and listen to Him in such a way that I could truly grow to be 'one with Him'.

Final Thoughts

Remember, learning to converse, even in human terms, is very much a learning process and all of us are different and unique in the way we talk with people and the same applies all the more strongly with God. There are, however, certain things that we can always bear in mind when we are thinking about conversing with God.

Be Careful . . .

All the stories I have given in this book are, of necessity, accounts of times when God has responded to a prayer or broken in to someone's thoughts. They are all positive and exciting stories but it is only fair to point out that there will be many times when God does not speak to us in this way. The

Psalms are full of people pouring their hearts out to God, using phrases like 'earnestly I seek you . . .'

Just as it is not always right for a mother to tell her child her reasons for everything, so it is not always right, or wise, for God to tell us everything. Jesus said that the kingdom of God could be likened to someone finding treasure in a field. In their joy they sell everything to buy that one field. I believe that God wants us to have that same joy when we think about hearing His voice. It will not happen everyday but when we do hear something it will be as precious as finding treasure.

The heart of all that God communicates with us has already been laid out and expressed in His Word, the Bible. There have been many cults and heresies that have sprung up as a result of people claiming to have had a direct word from God. On examination, however, this 'word from God' has proved to be in direct opposition to what the Bible teaches. Thousands have been deceived in this way. Morally too, people have claimed to have heard God tell them to do something that is totally different to what God has already told us to do in His Word. I read of a curate just the other day who declared God told him it was right to leave his wife and go off with another woman in the church! The more we drink in God's character and ways as we read His Word the more likely it will be that we hear Him correctly and not just according to our own desires.

Having said that, it is also important to realise that we will make mistakes. Just as we mishear and misunderstand each other, so we will mishear and misunderstand God. The disciples did all the time when Jesus was with them and the letters of Paul show that even when they had the Holy Spirit, they could still make mistakes. I do all the time. I remember once being convinced that God had told me we were going to go to Jamaica to sing. I had met a man whose brother was a lay preacher there and I was sure the Lord was telling me that He had brought this connection about Himself. I wrote to this man very enthusiastically only to be brought down to earth with a bump when he expressed no interest whatsoever!

How God Speaks when we Converse with Him

To start with, because God **is God** and not man, although He does want us to enter into real communication with Him, He will never talk in the vague, meandering way that makes up so much of our own conversations. Every word that God speaks, even if it is to give us wisdom in the kind of mundane situation that Marilyn was in with her jelly, will be full of point and purpose.

Throughout this chapter I have used phrases like 'a thought came into my mind', 'a voice said', 'an idea came'.

God met with Elijah when he was upset and traumatised by his experience with the Baal worshippers, He brought him out to see His glory and to hear His voice. But when God did speak it was not in the earthquake or wind, but in the tiny whisper. God speaks to us in that same 'still small voice' that He used then. We have been given the mind of Christ which is why when He does speak to us, it is like a whisper of a thought nudging us in our mind, a fleeting impression, a persistent idea. Just as I only hear a little bit of what someone says and often repeat back what I think I've heard in order for them to clarify it more to me, so we may have only a tiny idea at first of what God may be saying to us. We may have a verse come to mind, or a picture, or just an impression of specific words. Whatever comes to us we can give back to God – 'Lord I get the sense that you are saying . . . but I don't really know what it means/if it is you.' He says, 'All who seek will find me.' If we honestly want His word to be made clear to us He will show us and give us His peace.

OVER TO YOU

In the stories I've shared in this chapter I've given examples of times when people have prayed specifically for God to speak to them and other times when God has suddenly broken in. God will want to do it both ways as necessary and we need to have that heart belief and expectancy that He will want to speak to us, just because He is our Father.

1 When you have your quiet time, as well as bringing your needs and requests to Him, get your mind into an 'in tune' setting by praying something like Samuel's prayer 'Speak, Lord, for your servant is listening.'
2 If you are reading the Bible, or meditating on creation, or in a situation where the gifts of the Spirit are being used: if anything catches your attention in a particular way, like a phrase in a verse, or the beginning of a picture . . . talk to God about it. You could say something like 'Lord, this seems important but I don't know why. What are you trying to tell me?' Wait and expect that He will give you ideas to make the first thought more clear. If they come, do it again, give them back to Him and ask for even more understanding, just like you do in a normal conversation. If nothing comes don't worry, it may be He wants to show you more at a later point.
3 Maybe you have got a lot of worries on your mind, or maybe you are emotionally wounded by hurtful memories. When Joyce Huggett leads her quiet days and retreats, she encourages people in these situations to talk about the problems with the Lord, to picture the old memory, the hurtful person, the frustrating situation and then to say to the Lord, 'Lord, what do you think about this? How do you view this person or situation?' Then wait in an attitude of expectancy. Quite often, even when we are not waiting or meditating particularly God will still be trying to break in to our fretful

thoughts. It may just be a little nudge inside: 'I shouldn't really be thinking this, God does say He'll supply my every need after all . . .'

Instead of glossing over that and thinking 'Yes, but . . .' try saying to God, 'Lord you know I can hardly believe you'll even care about my needs let alone meet them . . . please teach me the truth!' and then, waiting and reading the Bible for His answer.

4 Whatever happens, whether you hear anything specifically or not, keep on talking with Him and seeking to understand and know Him better. Always thank Him that He's heard you and is answering you because God, unlike people, will never ignore you or be too busy to listen to you. If He doesn't appear to answer still thank Him because with God, silence doesn't mean no, but, not yet – wait.

PART 3

Listening in Prayer and Ministry

7
Creative Prayer and Intercession

Meeting with an Artist

A couple of years ago, Marilyn and I were visiting a lady artist called Annie.

'I just want to paint you each a personal picture as a little memento,' she said, after lunch.

Excited, we crowded round her at the easel. She was doing mine first and I watched her with fascination. I had never seen an artist at work before.

She stood thinking for a few minutes and then lifted a pen and started. As line after line went on in quickly executed strokes I couldn't tell what it was. Confidently she added more lines and filled in some with colour. Suddenly I gasped as I recognised myself in the cartoon-character style Annie is famous for, standing against a scenic background. One moment it had just been a blank sheet and the next an excellently drawn picture. She signed it with a flourish and handed it to me and now it hangs proudly over my bed at home.

An Idea Becomes Reality

Before Annie started, she had a picture in her mind of what she wanted to draw, but until she picked up her pen and started to put lines and shading on the paper, it was simply an idea and nothing more. As she drew, the idea was translated into visual reality on the page.

This is the same for everything creative. When we cook we have an idea in our minds of what we want to make, even if it is only a sandwich and we act in such a way that the idea becomes reality. The DIY expert sees in his mind's eye how he wants the new kitchen to look and cuts the work surfaces and designs the layout of the cupboards accordingly. Writing, music and design all follow the same principle.

What we are used to experiencing and practising in our daily lives, can also become a part of our prayer life, we can learn to be creative in our prayers, that what we long for in our hearts can be translated into reality as we pray.

Futile Prayers

Have you ever experienced praying and praying yet never seeming to get any answer? Everything you pray hits the ceiling, it just feels like empty words and you're not even sure if what you're praying is actually God's will?

I've been in that position many times and each time feel frustratedly that there must be some better way of praying. Not just repeating requests over and over but meeting with God in such a way that I know how to pray as well as what to pray. One night this did happen.

When I first knew Marilyn, she had dreadful back trouble and could hardly walk. She had all kinds of treatment and many people all over the country were praying for her healing but it just seemed to get worse. I was distressed when I saw her suffering so much and longed for God to heal her, but my prayers just seemed to hit the ceiling.

One night I cried out to God in desperation just before going to sleep, 'Lord, your Word seems to indicate that you want to heal but Marilyn is just getting worse! You say all we have to do is ask and it will be given us, but we've asked so many times and nothing has happened. I just don't know how to pray! If you do want to heal her please show me how to pray, Lord.'

That night I had a dream, a very simple one.

Marilyn and I were walking up Watford High Street, shopping. I had never actually done that with Marilyn because all she'd been able to walk, since I'd known her, was the few steps from the van into the church we were singing in.

In the dream we started at the very top of the High Street and were making our way to the bottom, about a mile. We were criss-crossing backwards and forwards over the road, looking at different shops. Marilyn was standing straight, not twisted sideways as she usually was, and was walking lightly and easily at my side. We were both talking and laughing all the way and I woke just as we reached the bottom end.

On waking the dream was still in my mind, in clear, vivid, detail. I was surprised by this as I invariably forgot my dreams. It seemed strange too that I'd dreamt about doing something so ordinary with Marilyn but which I hadn't actually experienced. Normally my dreams were more bizarre and unreal.

If only it could be true, I thought, seeing in my mind's eye Marilyn's shuffling painful walk.

It was then that the thought came to me, but it wasn't even a thought in the normal sense, certainly no words, just a sudden deep knowing right in my heart.

'This wasn't just a dream, this is what is going to happen.'

Well, that's amazing, I thought excitedly. Could that be what they describe as a prophetic dream? It will be wonderful when it does happen, I so hope it's soon. I swung my legs over the side of the bed and again, an impression, a knowing, came to me deep inside.

'You need to pray it into reality!'

I stood still, wondering if I could have imagined this, but the thought was still there. Yes this was a prophetic dream but I needed to pray it into reality. How could I do that? I wasn't sure but I knew that if this was going to be a way of praying that would help Marilyn then I wanted to try it.

Over the next few weeks and months I recalled this dream to my mind every day, sometimes when I was specifically praying and at other times when I saw that Marilyn was in a lot of pain. As the months went by and she got no better, my excitement, and even to a degree, my positive faith, disappeared and yet something within me made me cling onto that dream. Every time I felt like giving up in despair, the Lord seemed to remind me of it again and so I continued. Day after day I thanked the Lord that He was working in Marilyn's back, releasing the nerves that were trapped, bathing the inflammation, bringing about that lightness and freedom she had shown when walking in the dream. I tried to consciously see her standing and walking without pain and although I still hadn't been anywhere with her, I thanked the Lord that we would one day be walking up that High Street together.

About five months after I had the dream Marilyn's back got to the point where she knew she could no longer carry on. It was then, in a series of amazing steps, that the Lord began to turn things round. On her way down to Cornwall to do what was probably to be the last lot of concerts, Marilyn was in so much pain she cried out to the Lord to help her. Suddenly a strange thought seemed to come to her mind.

'When you get to Cornwall you are going to meet a Christian chiropractor who will be able to help you.'

Marilyn was startled. The thought was so definite, could it have been God? But no, it couldn't have been. She'd had some problems with chiropractors and was sure the Lord wouldn't want her to go to one of them. Maybe it was an osteopath she was going to meet?

When we had settled in at our hosts', Marilyn asked them casually, 'You don't happen to know of a Christian osteopath round here do you?'

'Not an osteopath,' Sue said, 'But we do know of a Christians chiropractor. He is coming tonight to hear you sing!'

Marilyn was dumbfounded and sure now that her thought had come from the Lord. Reg, the chiropractor, treated her several times while we were in Cornwall and after we returned home rang to say that he and his wife, Joy, wanted Marilyn to come and stay with them and he would treat her free of charge for as long as it took to get her back on her feet again. Deeply touched by this evidence of God's loving hand, Marilyn and I stayed there for six weeks and every day Reg treated her, praying for her at the same time.

Two months after, I was in Watford High Street one day with Marilyn. We had started out at the top end and after spending a lot of time crossing backwards and forwards between the shops, were now getting near the bottom. Marilyn was laughing about something when all of a sudden I stopped. I had that unmistakable sense of *déjà vu*. Then I remembered, of course, the dream! With a deep sense of amazement and awe I turned and looked back where we had just come from, and then at Marilyn. Gone was that agonised twisted walk, she still had a way to go and couldn't lift heavy things yet, but already there was that straightness and freedom that God had inspired me to pray for for so long. In just a few more yards we reached the bottom and the dream was fulfilled!

Our Creator God

Sometime after this I was doing a daily reading in Genesis. From the very first verse I was struck by something I had read thousands of times but had never realised the significance of before. That God brought the entire universe into being simply by speaking. That faced by the absolute nothingness and desolation of empty space, God just spoke and His very words were full of such a creative life and power that step by awesome step His plan for the universe was brought into reality. 'The earth was without form and an empty waste and darkness was upon the face of the very great deep' (Gen. 1:2 [Amplified Version]).

I got up and drew the curtains and closed my eyes tightly. I sat motionless and struggled to imagine the sheer totality of the emptiness and isolation, the pressing, heavy darkness, the absence of every form of life. Then the voice, shattering the darkness, piercing the night, searing through the atmosphere in a cosmic surge of power. 'God said "let there be light" and there was light' (Gen. 1:3).

Just a voice, not even shouted, just spoken, but bringing about unimaginable transformation. The voice of God, creating life out of nothingness, light out of darkness, fruitfulness out of barrenness, beauty out of ugliness. 'The universe was formed at God's command, so that what is seen was not made out of what was visible' (Heb. 11:3).

As I read these verses over and over it seemed as if a profound truth was beginning to shape itself in my heart. That when I had that dream for Marilyn followed by the urge to pray it into reality, God was doing the same thing through me as when He created the universe by speaking.

'But how could that be?' I thought, overwhelmed and awed by this thought. After all, I was praying to God when the dream came to me, but God *is* God so He just speaks and something happens.

I turned to the New Testament part of my daily reading, hoping I would find more illumination there. I was amazed at what I found. The opening verses seemed to speak to me again. 'In the beginning was the Word, and the Word was with God, and the Word was God. He was with God in the beginning. Through Him all things were made; without Him nothing was made that has been made' (John 1:1–3). 'Yet to all who received Him, to those who believed in His name, He gave the right to become children of God' (John 1:12).

As I thought about these verses it seemed as if the Lord Jesus Himself was standing next to me, directing my thoughts, speaking to me through each verse.

'You see, I was that very "Word" that was spoken each time something was created', He seemed to say. 'l was the power that made the universe come into being and I am the same one who was here as a man, died on the cross and rose again. Because you have believed in me you are now a child of God. I, the Word through whom all things were made am now living within you, through my Holy Spirit and that is the same Spirit that you have just read about in Genesis as "brooding over the waters" directly involved with creation.'

I got up from my chair and paced around the room as I strove to grasp hold of the truth of these thoughts and put them in order. Could it be that because I had the very life of Jesus inside me, the life of the one who is the actual 'Word of God', I could speak something into being just as God had spoken creation into being? That the way I had prayed for Marilyn was not just a one-off event but could be a way of enriching and empowering my whole prayer life? That prayer needn't just be me speaking repetitive, pleading words, but words that were full of the creative power of God?

I remembered the verse in Matthew where Jesus instructs us about prayer. 'And when you pray, do not keep on babbling like pagans, for they think they will be heard because of their many words. Do not be like them, for your Father knows what you need before you ask Him' (Matt. 6:7–8).

I suddenly realised that in my early desperation for Marilyn to be healed I had lost all sense of God's character, of His faithfulness and His love for Marilyn as her Father. All I could think of was the problem, and so my prayers were just repetitions of a hope but I had no real faith that anything would happen.

But surely, I thought, there was another occasion in Luke 11 where Jesus told the story about the man who keeps badgering his friend for bread late at night because he has had an unexpected visitor. At first the friend is a bit reluctant but as the man persists Jesus concludes with this comment, 'because of the man's boldness he will get up and give him as much as he needs' (Luke 11:8).

I was puzzled by these two stories. The first seemed to show that many words were not needed, the second that persistence in asking was needed. Wasn't that just a contradiction? Again it seemed as if the Lord was revealing something to me which I hadn't recognised before. The man in the second example persisted in his request with 'boldness' because he had come to a friend for help. He wasn't just repeating words over and over but was trusting in his knowledge of his friend's character which enabled him to be bold, even when the friend seemed reluctant at first.

It seemed as if the Holy Spirit was saying to me:

> 'Just as he went to a friend in his need so you are coming to a friend. That is why you can ask boldly, because the more you get to know God as your friend and Father, the more you will have a heart understanding of His will and what He wants to do for you and through you, and so you will learn to pray with that same boldness.'

God Reveals His purposes

Excited by these thoughts and longing to discover more, I continued searching for anything that could give me more understanding. Immediately, I discovered that following the creation, God always chose to bring His purposes about through man's involvement, as if He had planned from the very beginning for us to be a partner in His plans. Again and again I saw God giving His people a fleeting glimpse, through dreams, or prophecy, or pictures, of what He was going to do for them and as they responded in prayer, or obedient action, bringing that promise about.

Abraham – an Individual!

When Abraham was sad at the prospect of not having an heir God led him to look at the stars and try to count them. 'Then He said to him, "so shall your offspring be"' (Gen. 15:5). Thus God responded to Abraham's own personal need while at the same time giving him a picture promise of national and eternal significance.

The Israelites – a Nation

When the Israelites were suffering under the tyranny of the Egyptians, God heard their cries and responded by making Himself known to Moses. He gave Moses a verbal picture of the new land He was going to give them. 'And I have come down to deliver them out of the hand and power of the Egyptians and to bring them up out of that land to a land good and large, a land flowing with milk and honey, a land of plenty . . .' (Exod. 3:8 [Amplified Version]).

As they escaped from the Egyptians, Moses spoke of this picture as a living reality until it became, not just his picture, but the future of all the people.

The Coming Messiah

Hundreds of years before Jesus came, God spoke through the prophets revealing the nature and purpose of the coming Messiah and giving the Israelites an incredible vision of what to pray, and wait for, in joyful expectation. 'For to us a child is born, to us a son is given, and the government will be on His shoulders. And He will be called Wonderful Counsellor, Mighty God, Everlasting Father, Prince of Peace. Of the increase of His government and peace there will be no end' (Isa. 9:6–7).

I saw that those who had a true love and reverence for God

and were full of the Holy Spirit, took up these pictures, warnings and prophecies and made them their own permanent heart-felt prayer. Passing on the vision from one generation to another, praying, believing, responding and obeying until they became reality.

Treasuring God's Word in our Hearts

In the New Testament it tells how the angel came to Joseph to reassure him about the divine nature of Mary's pregnancy. As the angel spoke, a word picture was communicated to Joseph of what he was to expect for his son, 'you are to give Him the name Jesus, because He will save His people from their sins' (Matt. 1:21).

Following the birth, an old man called Simeon (Luke 2:25–35) gave Mary and Joseph another word picture of the future, '"This child is destined to cause the falling and rising of many in Israel"' (Luke 2:34).

Luke records that after these amazing events Mary, a simple peasant girl, 'treasured all these things in her heart' (Luke 2:19).

It is this act of 'treasuring in the heart' that forms the foundation of our prayers, especially this kind of creative, listening prayer. In his book *Prayer, Key to Revival* Paul Yonggi Cho tells how in his early poverty stricken days as a young pastor, he was in desperate need of some basic items, a table and chair to enable him to study, and a bicycle. Months passed as he kept praying for these things without any sign of God providing them. One day, feeling very frustrated, he asked God why He didn't seem to be fulfilling His promise to meet all our needs and an answering thought came into his mind that God, because He loved him as a Father, wanted him to be more specific about the kind of table, chair and bicycle he wanted. Cho responded to this, and picturing in his imagination how he wanted each thing to look, prayed specifically thanking God that those things would soon be part of his life. The bicycle he asked for was an American make, virtually impossible to obtain in South Korea, but at the end of one week all three items were delivered to his house and all three were just as he'd prayerfully imagined them.

The Desires of our Hearts

When I read stories like Cho's or hear similar testimonies I often feel, 'How can we know that what we're praying for, and trying to speak into reality, is right for us? Suppose it's just our own selfish desires?' Deep down I feel that if I really want something, it can't possibly be right because God is bound to want something different! Sometimes I have refrained completely from praying for something because I feel so sure of this.

While it is true that we are easily tempted to go rushing after the wrong things and we often have the wrong motives, I am coming to believe that the closer we get to God, the more we dwell on His love letters to us (the Bible!) and spend time talking to Him, listening to Him, and worshipping Him, the more our desires and longings, and even our very thoughts, will come in line with His. He knows our hearts and even if we haven't got it right, if we are earnestly seeking Him, He will know how to change us.

I remember the very first time I went on holiday with Marilyn. For the first few days we spent most of our time trying to find out what each other wanted to do. Our conversation would go something like this:

Marilyn: 'What would you like to do now, we could go swimming, or get a boat, or look round the shops a bit . . .?'

Tracy: 'Oh I don't mind, I'm happy with anything. I suppose we could swim now, but if you'd rather . . . !'

And so on and on . . .

Half an hour later we would discover that we'd both originally fancied doing the same thing anyway! The thing is, we were already friends and, as most friends or couples do, had grown to love doing similar things. But we couldn't believe that the other would be happy if we said directly what we wanted to do! This is how we often approach God, yet there is a wonderful verse in Psalm 37 that shows how much God is longing to fulfil our desires. 'Delight yourself also in the Lord and He will give you the desires and secret petitions of your heart' (Ps. 37:4 [Amplified Version]).

In fact, the wonderful thing is, that it is often the Lord who has put the desires there in the first place. As this story will illustrate.

Many have been blessed over the last decade by the healing ministry and training at Ellel Grange Conference Centre in Lancashire. I visited Ellel soon after it started and was amazed to hear how God had brought it about. Peter Horrobin, now the overall director of Ellel Ministries was a thirty-year-old technical publisher when God spoke to him one night. Peter was praying with someone who had been sexually abused. He was finding it difficult for he had no knowledge or training in the healing ministry. After the person had left, God gave Peter a vision showing how he was to spend the rest of his life ministering healing to those in need and training others to do it. This seemed crazy to Peter because of his lack of experience, but he knew without any doubt that it was from God.

Peter prayed into that vision for ten years. There was no tangible evidence that it was ever going to happen, but daily Peter asked God to give him understanding and knowledge, and greater vision of how this calling should be brought about. Daily, God answered Peter's prayer and as the knowledge came to him, Peter prayed it into reality. By the time God led him to Ellel Grange ten years later, all Peter had learnt and prayed came into focus as the first 'healing retreats' began.

Since that time, a second centre, Glyndley Manor, has been

established in Sussex, together with centres in Canada and Eastern Europe, amongst others. Each time God has given Peter, and the other directors, a vision of a new area of expansion, and as they've prayed it into reality, and stepped out in faith, He has brought it about.

Faith Comes from Hearing

When we have truly heard God, either through a dream or vision 'type' of experience, or a little inward thought, or a Bible verse taking on a new life as we read it, faith is born in our hearts. That is why Paul says 'faith comes through hearing the message, and the message is heard through the word of Christ' (Rom. 10:17). Hearing Him brings that deep inner knowing that enables us to pray with real creative certainty.

In March 1989 we were travelling to Poland for a tour when Marilyn started sharing with me how depressed she felt because she wasn't getting any ideas for new songs but she was under contract to make a new album that December.

'I just don't know what to do,' she sighed, 'I keep praying and meditating and asking the Lord for inspiration but my mind's a complete blank. I feel I've come to the end of my creativity. Maybe I'm not meant to be writing any more songs!'

I could not believe that was true and that night after Marilyn was asleep I started to talk to Jesus about it. 'Lord, please give her the ideas she needs, or if it's not your will that she writes any more, please show her.'

I stopped, frustrated. This was one of those prayers again where I was just waffling round in circles not even sure if what I was praying was right! Moreover, for some strange reason my thoughts kept flitting to my friend who happened to be pregnant. 'Can't you even keep your mind on what you're meant to be praying about,' I scolded myself. But even as I was thinking that, an awareness began to grow within me, as if my thoughts were being led in a new direction. My frustration lifted as I sensed deep inside that God my Father was with me and speaking to me. First of all I felt an inner peace that God had heard my prayers and that Marilyn was meant to still be writing songs, and then I had an amazing idea.

'Just as your friend is pregnant, it is as if Marilyn is pregnant,' the Lord seemed to be saying. 'As she has prayed to me I have planted the seeds of ideas and lyrics in her spirit just like the egg that is planted in the mother's womb. Like the mother in her earliest weeks of pregnancy there is no obvious sign of growth yet but those seeds have taken root and will grow and develop into the songs I want them to become, just as the foetus develops in its allotted time, into a perfectly formed child.'

That's wonderful, I thought, I can't wait to tell Marilyn, what an encouragement! But once again I found myself thinking something that I knew could only be the Holy Spirit directing me.

I mustn't tell Marilyn yet, but instead, I must pray through her pregnancy of songs. I must prayerfully visualise them growing within her, see each part coming into place just like a baby.

The months went by quickly and still there was no sign of any songs. Each month I continued praying, visualising those songs within her like a growing baby, praying for the Holy Spirit to fill her and feed her with creativity just as a baby is fed by its mother. September came and still nothing. I wondered if I was mad but it was the only way I could think of praying, so I carried on.

October, a few vague ideas but nothing concrete. I'd been praying eight and a half months. November was one of our busiest months, I couldn't see how she was going to do it. Suddenly, out of the blue we suddenly found ourselves with three weeks of concerts being cancelled, all for different reasons. We'd never had such a thing happen before.

'I suppose I should try and write some songs,' Marilyn said, switching on the keyboard. I went to do some cleaning and an hour later went back in to find her pounding away excitedly.

'I've had an idea,' she called, 'quick, get me my tape recorder, it's really coming together!'

Over those next three weeks, exactly nine months after that prayer direction from God, I could only watch in awe and amazement as Marilyn wrote song after song, eventually completing fourteen just in time for the recording.

A Creative Relationship with God

Most of the stories and biblical examples so far have been to do with our need to pray or intercede for some situation or individual, but what about when we are coming to God in our own personal worship? There have been many occasions when I have found it almost impossible to come to God in prayer. Times when I have been so aware of my failures and shortcomings that I can't believe He will really love me, and even if He does I can't feel it. Talking to my friends, and people that come up for ministry at the end of a concert, shows that this isn't just my problem but one that many people have.

I remember Mary sobbing out her belief that God could never really love her when we were praying about the long buried guilt of her abortion. Jane in tears, who when I said, 'God will forgive you,' answered, 'Yes, I know He will in my head, but I can't feel it.' I remember too, Lesley, who I had thought was a perfectly happy Christian, saying to Marilyn and me one afternoon, 'You know I just don't know how to come to God as Father! Because of what my Dad did to me, I dare not trust myself to Him even though I am saying I do!'

What I feel is so wonderful though, is the fact that God our Father shows in His Word, that He understands that we sometimes need more than just cold words or determination, we need a 'mind picture' of what He is like and how He will receive us, and what He will do for us. And our God is a God who delights in pictures. Just looking through the stories in the Gospels the other day brought that fact to life again for me. I saw Jesus telling us that we can ask God for good gifts as simply and as boldly as a child asking his dad for food; the father welcoming home his delinquent son, not just with a formal handshake, but a loving embrace followed by a party; the traveller, beaten up, rejected and left for dead by the passers by, yet rescued by a man who uses his own clothes to bind his wounds, his own money to get him shelter and who ensures he is cared for until he is better.

Words like 'light', 'fountains and streams', 'shepherd', 'rock and fortresses', 'everlasting arms' are used again and again to give us a graphic picture of what God is like and what He wants to do for us. But the exciting and awe-inspiring thing is that they are not just nice descriptive words, but words that are full of the very life and power of God and have the power to bring about within us the very thing they are describing.

Brother Lawrence, the seventeenth-century monk famous for his book *The Practice of the Presence of God*, tells how he used to have a very deep sense of his own sin and worthlessness before God. Reading the Bible one day, he came to the Parable of the Wedding Feast. In his imagination he saw himself going to that feast, hesitating on the threshold, aware of his filthy, stinking clothes. Then the king drawing him in, giving him a beautiful white robe and wonderful food. As Lawrence imagined this and talked to the Lord about it he realised that his feelings of worthlessness were being replaced by a deep joy and peace.

The writer and speaker, Joyce Huggett, well known for her many books especially *Listening to God*, ministers to people by encouraging them to come to God in this imaginative way.

Marilyn and I went to see her for a fortnight's guided retreat.

I soon became aware that a lot of fears were still binding me emotionally. Fears of failing, fears of what people would think of me, fears of stepping out into new things. As I prayed, I felt too paralysed to even imagine coming out of the deep, inner shell where part of me had been hiding for years.

Joyce prayed quietly with me and then suggested that I meditate on the story of Jesus raising Lazarus from the dead and try to put myself in Lazarus' shoes, as if it was me lying bound up in that tomb suddenly hearing the call of Jesus to live again.

When I was alone, I read the passage through, then lay back on my bed and closed my eyes. As Joyce had suggested, I engaged all my senses, imagining the hard rock, the thick shroud binding me from head to toes, the heavy pressing darkness all around. As I imagined each thing I asked the Lord to reveal to me any areas of my life these things might be symbolically representing. What was it that was binding me like that shroud? Was there some kind of tomb door locking me in and shutting out the light? As I prayed, ideas came to my mind in response which I acknowledged without trying to deal with there and then. Again, I imagined Lazarus lying so dead, alone and cut off from all hope and the voice of God suddenly piercing through the suffocating darkness with the command to 'Come out'. Lying on my bed I felt that sick fear gripping me again and I prayed that what Jesus had done for Lazarus He would do for me. I lay still, silent, alone, afraid like a tiny child and it was then that I 'heard' Jesus calling me. It was like a clear, vivid thought spreading through my mind, accompanied by a deep peaceful knowing, that this wasn't just me trying to reconstruct a Bible passage but it was God speaking to me in person.

'Tracy, choose life, you are beautiful to me. Choose to be the woman you are.'

As God's call entered my spirit and bathed my mind and heart it brought with it the realisation that I could change,and that I wanted to. There and then I said to Jesus, 'I will choose . . .' Like Lazarus I was not free of the bonds yet, but something was changed within me.

Just like the disciples had to remove Lazarus' shroud for him, so Joyce then prayed for me to be released from every emotional or mental shroud that had been binding me. And even as she prayed I could feel a deep releasing happening, as if I could see life with new eyes and anticipate enjoying things I'd always feared. Interestingly, Joyce's husband David, who knew nothing about what had been happening, commented later when we were out for a meal together, that he'd never seen me look so alive.

Getting Started

Inevitably, we often come to God in the midst of our problems, often feeling weary and hopeless, only able to see the mountain of difficulties that is weighing us down. We tell Him about it and ask Him to help us. Unfortunately, what I, and many of us, often do then is get up and carry on with my life without stopping to hear what God might want to tell me. But how many of us would rattle off a problem to a close friend and then get up and walk out of the room before he/she has had a chance to answer? Jesus said, 'Seek and you will find me.' To seek means a real whole-hearted opening up of ourselves to God, persevering in prayer, giving Him time to answer. As David expresses in Psalm 40, 'I waited patiently and expectantly for the Lord and He inclined to me and heard my cry' (Ps. 40:1 [Amplified Version]).

We won't always get an answer straight away. There will be many times when the Lord holds back and teaches us to wait, and maybe to ask for a different thing, but remember that what I am talking about is not a quick, instant fix to a problem but the wisdom to know how to pray about that problem, and as

James says, 'God loves to give us wisdom without finding fault!' (Jas. 1:5). Often all we will get at the initial stage is a little inward nudge, an idea, a flash of insight, a sudden thought or inner feeling. As we carry on praying this back to God, He will draw us closer to His heart and understanding, and so bring us to that point where we can receive a more specific picture like a dream, vision or prophetic message. He will speak this deep inside us, so that it is a secret between us and God, one that we treasure in our hearts, see with our imaginations and, remembering that the very 'Word of God' is alive within us, pray into reality.

OVER TO YOU

Creative Intercession

If you have a burden for a person, a situation, an area or an event, or a deep longing to see God working, His transforming power released, His love poured out, then you need to know how He wants you to pray in order for His will and creative life to be fully released through your prayers.

1 First of all seek Him in His Word to ensure that what you are praying for is in line with His general, revealed will. As you read, remembering that the Bible is not just rules and theories, but the very life and power of God, ask the Holy Spirit to give you the mind of Christ, making alive any verse or passage through which He wants to speak to you.
2 Keep lifting the person or situation into the Lord's 'everlasting arms' and praying that the Lord's will be brought about for them.
3 Ask the Lord specifically to give you wisdom to know how to pray. Then wait on Him with an expectant attitude.
4 If you sense God is answering you, maybe through a specially

significant Bible verse, a dream, vision, unusual idea or sequence of thoughts . . . give it back to Jesus asking Him to confirm, with His gift of peace in your spirit, if it really is how He wants you to pray. Once you have that certainty, start to pray what He has shown you into reality.

5 If there does not seem to be any specific word at this time keep waiting on God and lifting the situation up to Him. Ask Him to reveal and transform any wrong motives you may have and be confident that your prayers are being heard by your loving Heavenly Father who loves to give to those who seek Him, and who has all things in His hands.

6 Even if you haven't received a specific way of praying, you can still pray creatively by taking a Bible picture, appropriate to the situation, and imaginatively praying into it. For example, if your friend is under strain from overwork or family pressures, you could prayerfully imagine the Holy Spirit as that 'Stream of Living Water' flowing gently through the dry areas of her life, bringing renewal and new fruit where there has only been barrenness. If a husband and wife are fighting you could pray for that 'oneness' which is God's desire for every marriage. If someone is pulled down by many fears you could prayerfully imagine them standing securely on Christ, the Rock which can never be shaken. If an area, or country, is becoming more and more ruled by cruelty, hardness and spiritual darkness, you could prayerfully imagine the light of Jesus which overcomes the blackest of all darknesses, beginning to fill the streets. The name of Jesus lifted high on a banner, the 'Sword of the Spirit' wielded against every 'Roaring lion' manifestation of evil. Jesus described the needy world as a field of ripening corn and told us to pray with this picture in our minds, that the Lord of the harvest will send out workers – Christians – into the harvest field – the world.

These are just a few examples but the Bible is full of such

pictures and they all express the revealed will of God. As we pray them into the situation, the transforming power of God is released.

I believe it was the 'Lydia Intercessory Prayer' newsletter that told the story of how Christians began to pray for a notoriously red-light area in Amsterdam, specifically concentrating on the sex and pornographic shops in one particular street. As they prayed, they imagined the potential customers becoming blind to the goods. They prayed for God's light and holiness to fill each site instead of the evil darkness and perversion, and they prayerfully 'saw' the shop interiors filled with beautiful God-glorifying things. They could only praise God when, in a matter of about five weeks, three of the shops had closed down and when they reopened, amongst other things, one had become a florist and another a Christian bookstore.[1]

Personal Prayer

1 Find a place where you can be on your own with Jesus. Thank Him for His forgiveness and His love. Thank Him that He is your Father who is always with you. Consciously lift any immediate worries or fears into His hands. Ask the Holy Spirit to come and open your ears and be your counsellor.
2 Choose one of the many parable stories that Jesus told, e.g. Lazarus, the Prodigal Son, the Good Samaritan, the Wedding Feast.
3 Put yourself into that person's shoes. For example, imagine yourself as that weary traveller in the Good Samaritan story. See the blackness of the road, hear the sound of the men creeping up on you. Ask yourself, and the Lord, if there's any symbolic dark road you have been travelling. Have there been any events that have left you feeling overwhelmed or broken in your life? Become aware of any emotions filling

you, fear, grief, anger etc.

Imagine the traveller's feelings as each person approaches, the hope, the let-down, the rejection and growing sense of worthlessness. Imagine the Good Samaritan, Jesus, coming to you. His gentleness as He lifts you. In faith, see Him pouring out the balm of His Holy Spirit on your wounds and binding them up with His loving words. Acknowledge the cost this has been to Him, not just in money and time like the Good Samaritan, but in His very life. Realise that this is the depth of His love for you and He will never leave you or reject you. See how He ensures the traveller will be looked after until he is whole and imagine yourself entering into complete wholeness.

8
Listening to God in Ministry and Evangelism

Hearing how to Minister

Several years ago, my pastor Gordon and his wife Rachel were visiting Reinhard Bonnke's 'Christ for all Nations' team for a crusade in Harare.

At 10 p.m. one night, they had just returned from the crusade when they heard a terrific crash outside. A car had gone out of control and slammed into a Land Rover.

As they battled frantically to open its door they heard the sound of another vehicle speeding up behind them. They took no notice, the road was wide and they were easily visible. But suddenly the silence was shattered by a squeal of tyres. Rachel glanced round and screamed. A seven ton army truck was hurtling towards them. She froze, eyes clenched shut, spread-eagled against the car, then her body exploded in pain as the truck collided with a violent screech of ripping metal. Gordon was hurled several feet into a ditch, breaking his pelvis and spine. Rachel, caught between the two vehicles, was left with two shattered legs.

When we heard the news in England, the church elders immediately organised a twenty-four-hour prayer rota. We were told that Rachel had slipped into a terminal coma and that the doctors were saying it was unlikely she would recover consciousness. They gave her a 5 per cent chance of life and then only as a 'vegetable'.

While her parents, Alan and Eileen flew to be with her, the

church fasted and prayed night after night, seeking God for His will and word. 'Lord, show us how to pray!' was the prayer in all our hearts.

One night, about ten days after the accident a lady in the fellowship had a vision as we were waiting on the Lord. In the vision, she told us, she could see Rachel with a kind of clamp or chain all around her head. This lady sensed that God was saying that this clamp was the work of the devil who was trying to hold Rachel in death.

'Pray against the darkness of this spirit of death in My name,' God told her. 'Pray that the chains are loosened and broken and for my healing power and light to drive away the darkness, inside her head and brain as well as around it.'

With one heart and mind we began to pray in this way. We stripped away the darkness and the chains in the name of Jesus and with imaginative, graphic prayers, prayed God's healing light onto her head. As God led us, we prayed for the bruising and damage to her skull and brain to be bathed by the balm of the Holy Spirit.

As a fellowship we were all amazed and filled with awe when we heard the next day what had happened. Her mother, Eileen had gone to pray with Rachel at the same time as we were praying in the church. As she prayed she felt she needed to speak life and light into Rachel's brain and rebuke the hold of the devil. She continued praying in this way for quite some time and suddenly Rachel opened her eyes! She recognised her mother, was able to speak and there was no sign of any brain damage. When we realised what God had done, we cried with joy, but there was more to come.

When Gordon and Rachel eventually returned home, the church decided to hold a special healing service for Rachel. She told us that the doctors said the bones in her legs had been so shattered they weren't knitting together again properly and it was unlikely she would ever walk normally again. We all began to pray and, as before, asked the Lord to reveal His will and strategy to us.

Suddenly one of the leaders began to speak, 'I believe the Lord is leading me to Ezekiel 37,' he said. This is the story where Ezekiel is told to prophesy life and flesh into the dead bones: 'Then He said to me, "Prophesy to these bones and say to them, 'Dry bones, hear the word of the Lord! . . . I will make breath enter you, and you will come to life'"' (Ezek. 37:4–6).

He paused and we all waited expectantly, 'I believe the Lord wants us to prophesy the same thing over Rachel's legs. This isn't just a story. It is the very word and power of God. I believe that as we pray in this way, God will make His Word real for Rachel and the dry bones of her legs will be healed.'

A wave of joy and faith rolled over us as we came around Rachel to pray for her. Taking the words of the Bible we spoke them out as we laid hands on her legs. We prophesied over them: 'Dry, broken bones, become whole in the name of Jesus and you will stand and walk and run again.'

After a repeat meeting the following week and a check-up at the hospital, Rachel told us the exciting news. Against all the doctors' expectations the miracle was happening, all the bones were knitting back together and healing had begun.

God continued to give Rachel faith that He would complete this healing. One night, four years after the accident, she sensed Him saying to her: 'The time for healing has come.' Shortly after that, a pastor commanded her leg to twist back and lengthen one and a half inches. It happened! For the first time since the accident she was able to stand straight with both heels on the ground. Today, over ten years since the accident, Rachel walks, runs, dances without any trace of a limp!

Lord Teach us to Pray

Even as I was writing this story, I felt that same thrill of awe and praise at the greatness and love of God that we all felt during those eventful weeks. But as great as the miracle of healing itself, was the miracle of God showing us how He wanted us to pray and minister to Rachel. Listening to Him and finding out His strategy, not only gave us more faith, but was the difference between our prayers being mere words and the Word of God. Hearing His will gave us the sort of power that it describes in 2 Corinthians. 'For though we live in the world, we do not wage war as the world does. The weapons we fight with are not the weapons of the world. On the contrary they have divine power to demolish strongholds' (2 Cor. 10:3–4).

Jesus has called us to do the things He did that people might know He is alive. There is so much darkness and pain in all the world at this present time. We can feel overwhelmed when we hear of the terrible problems in the Third World, or read about the increase in violence in the papers, but what about when a friend or neighbour suffers a nervous breakdown or is diagnosed with cancer? Or when a lady at church shares how she has felt terrified of men since she was raped? What about the young insecure teenager who tells you bitterly that whatever he does no one ever likes him and there's no point him being a Christian because God would never bother with him either? These are the type of people you and I mix with all the time, just ordinary people with ordinary, but sometimes heartbreaking, problems.

When someone comes to me and starts talking about their problems I often panic. 'How can I possibly help,' I think, and make some trite sympathetic sounds: 'That's right,' 'Yes it's difficult isn't it . . .' 'Yes it's natural for you to feel that . . .' Inwardly I think 'This is hopeless, I must have better answers than that!' But in actual fact I haven't got any answers at all, and like the disciples, I need to learn to say, 'Lord, teach me to pray.'

Jesus wants us to be Whole

When I first became a Christian I had many emotional problems and none of them changed overnight. When I read verses like: 'O Lord, you have examined my heart and know everything about me' (Ps. 139:1 [Living Bible]), I felt afraid because I thought that if Jesus could really see my heart, how could He possibly still love me?

What I didn't realise was that when Jesus died that terrible death on the cross, He took with Him, not only my sin, but all my sorrows too: 'yet it was our grief He bore, our sorrows that weighed Him down' (Isa. 53:4 [Living]).

I did not understand that just as He had taken the heavy weight of my guilt and regrets and replaced it with a deep inner peace and freedom, so He also wanted to take the fears, the griefs and the painful memories and replace them with His healing love and joy. I remember when I read Isaiah 61 this truth suddenly opening up in all its meaning to me.

> The Spirit of the Sovereign Lord is on me, because the Lord has anointed me to preach good news to the poor. He has sent me to bind up the broken-hearted, to proclaim freedom for the captives and release from darkness for the prisoners . . . to comfort all who mourn, and provide for those who grieve . . . to bestow on them a crown of beauty instead of ashes, the oil of gladness instead of mourning, and a garment of praise instead of a spirit of despair. (Isa. 61:1–3)

Tears came to my eyes as I realised the depth of transformation the Lord had in mind for me. But although I had new hope that this is what God wanted to do, I had no idea how He could do it. After all, the past was past and how could I change my emotional habits of a lifetime? It was as my friends began to pray with me that I began to realise how Jesus heals our hearts.

John and Amanda knew virtually nothing about me that first night as I sat, typically hard and unresponsive, on their settee. They prayed quietly for the Holy Spirit to come and fill and direct us and waited a few moments in silence. Suddenly Amanda began to speak: 'I keep seeing you as a very young child. You are helpless and very afraid. You are alone and enclosed in an unfamiliar place.'

As she spoke it was as if a part of me deep down inside suddenly identified with this picture and I could see myself in that place, frightened and alone.

'That may have been the hospital when I was two,' I said.

'Well, Jesus wants to heal that memory,' said John. 'He wants to give you a new picture to replace that old fearful one. He calls Himself "I Am". Because He is eternal and not bound by time as we are, He can see you right now as you were then. We can ask Him to show Himself to you in such a way that the fear and loneliness that took hold of you will be melted away, because it says in the Bible that the perfect love of God drives away our fear.'

Praying softly, they asked the Lord to do this for me. For a long time all I was aware of was my fear. But suddenly it was as if I could see myself in that strange place. All the hostile, frightening things were surrounding me as before, but I was no longer alone. I could see, or rather, sense Jesus standing with me. For the first time since becoming a Christian I reached out to Him not just as an adult but as a child and, deep in that childish memory, I 'heard' Him promise me that He would never leave or forsake me (Heb. 13:5).

A deep level of healing began to take place in my life that night. It was not that the memories were being changed, that was impossible! It was that, as my friends made themselves available to God's leading and encouraged me to see or hear what He was doing or saying in each situation, my perception of the memories changed. I was able to open up to Jesus on a deeper level and allow His healing words to break the power of the negative, binding things that had happened. On each occasion my friends listened to see if there was any particular memory or area that God wanted us to focus on and how we should pray about it. Different situations like my Dad's illness and death, and some of the school traumas, were all opened up to us by God in this way.

Only Jesus has the Power . . . but He Gives it to Us!

The thing I find so wonderful, is that while psychologists and psychiatrists may have the knowledge and ability to dig up the roots of a problem, they have no power to actually deal with it. Jesus is the only One who can do that and He wants to teach us, as we listen to Him, to give His life-transforming love to others, just as my friends did for me.

Every time I read the Gospels I am deeply encouraged that Jesus, like ordinary man, needed to have constant communication with His Heavenly Father in order to fulfil His ministry. He spent a great deal of time on His own in prayer with God. He prayed before choosing His disciples, He prayed before every major decision about where to go. He prayed ceaselessly when surrounded by the crowds of needy people. Although the Bible account does not go into details of how He prayed, it is obvious that in each situation He received the wisdom to know what to do.

Many occasions are recorded of Him healing blind people, yet He did not heal them all in the same way. In most examples He touched their eyes but talked and prayed with them in different ways, according to what He sensed their needs were. In the famous story of the paralytic lowered through the roof by his determined friends, Jesus did not immediately minister physical healing but focused instead on the man's need for forgiveness. I am always amazed when I read this story. After all, it was so clear that it was for their friend to be healed that the four men went to such desperate lengths. But as Jesus heard the commotion of the roof being pulled apart above Him and then saw the man carefully lowered down, maybe He sent up one of those quick prayers: 'Father, I can see this man needs, and wants, healing but is there anything else he needs first? Is there a root cause of his sickness?'

And maybe the knowledge came back to Him: 'He has a long buried guilt which he needs to know he is forgiven for, then he will be able to receive physical healing.'

Possibly you are thinking right now, but of course Jesus would know how to minister to people, after all, He is God! But Jesus did not hold back when His disciples asked Him to teach them to pray, He taught them! He said that His sheep (us) would know His voice, and He prayed specifically that we would be one with Him just as He is one with the Father. So that means that in just the same way as Him, we can discern, as we pray and listen to Him, how to pray for someone. We can have the power to know whether it is the most obvious thing we should be praying for or something deeper.

Hearing the Root

I remember once, an elderly lady responded to a word of knowledge Marilyn had, saying that someone was in a great deal of pain. This lady had rheumatoid arthritis and she had not been able to lift her arms for twenty years. Both Marilyn and I felt nervous and inadequate. Neither of us had seen people healed physically through our prayers before and we didn't want her to be disappointed. Marilyn prayed, thanking Jesus that He loved and knew Doris and wanted the very best for her. She then asked the Holy Spirit to reveal to us how we should pray. In the quietness a thought came to me that she was feeling very guilty about something that had happened long ago. I prayed about this, asking the Lord if there was anything more specific. Nothing more came to mind but I felt a deep sense of peace that this was from Him. When I did eventually share this thought, Marilyn said that she'd had a sense that something had happened that had caused Doris a great deal of sorrow. Turning to her, she gently asked if these thoughts seemed right.

Doris began to weep, she struggled to wipe the tears away with her twisted hands and after a few moments began to speak.

'My daughter was raped twenty-five years ago, she was only thirteen.' She tried to control her voice. 'It was the baby-sitter, he was a family friend. I never thought . . . but I shouldn't have trusted him, I should have got a girl, I should have stayed at home. It's my fault and she's never recovered. So many years have gone by but her life has been ruined. I can't forgive myself for leaving her on her own with him.' She broke down again, her whole body shaking with sobs.

With our arms around her, Marilyn and I prayed quietly that Jesus would take away the years of despair and self-recrimination, break the power of the devil's lies and enable her to both forgive herself, and the man who had so betrayed her trust. Gradually the weeping lessened. In the end, at our encouragement, she prayed herself, accepting the Lord's forgiveness and love and laying the whole ugly memory and the present brokenness of her daughter's life in the Lord's hands.

After a long still pause she looked up, and we were amazed at the light shining in her eyes.

'I saw the Lord on the cross,' she whispered. 'He was looking at me with eyes so full of love. He seemed to be saying "Now you can live again, Doris . . ."'

There were tears in our eyes too. What a transformation from just a few moments ago!

We prayed briefly that the healing she'd received in her spirit would flow throughout every part of her life, especially her body and then said goodbye.

The next day our hostess had a phone call and burst into our room full of excitement.

'That was Doris,' she exclaimed. 'She said she got up this morning and was able to brush her hair and dress herself. She was even able to reach up to the high shelves in her larder for the first time in twenty years!'

Listen to Him

You see, just like that paralytic, Doris needed spiritual and emotional healing before she could be physically healed. Only Jesus knew what was happening in her heart and because He loved her so much He wanted her to be whole. If Marilyn and I had just rushed ahead with our own set way of praying, we wouldn't have got anywhere.

Soon after this incident I learned that doctors and psychologists agreed that rheumatoid arthritis was often caused by stress or problems that have not been dealt with. I was excited by this, realising it confirmed what had happened with Doris. A few weeks later we had another opportunity to pray with a lady with arthritis and with great enthusiasm I started questioning her about possible grief, anger or bitterness. She shook her head but, when I persisted, said huffily, 'I came up because I wanted the Lord to touch my body and help me with the pain and all you can do is accuse me of being bitter.'

She rose and as fast as she could on her swollen stiffened legs, walked away.

I felt terrible but a few weeks later made the same mistake. After this second disaster I went to the Lord in despair. I will never forget the gentle rebuke in His reply.

'I never speak once-for-all. The arthritis of the other people was purely a physical problem but you thought you knew all the answers. Why didn't you listen to me for them as you did with the first?'

There and then I asked the Lord to forgive me and help me not to just rely on theories but to seek Him for each individual. Although I still often make mistakes, especially when I am going through a dry period in my Christian life, I have a growing understanding that in order to be truly effective when ministering I need to hear His strategy each time.

But how do we Listen?

Hearing God at any time takes perseverance and practice. Hearing Him when faced by the clamour of someone's urgent need is even harder. This is where some of the principles I described in the last chapter can help. C. S. Lewis talks in one of his books of the 'baptised imagination' and I think this is a wonderful way of describing this kind of creative praying and ministering in faith.

We need to realise that when someone starts sharing with us, Jesus is actually close by us. Supporting us, empowering us and speaking through us. He is also close by the one you are about to pray for and has the same desire to speak to them as He has to you. Jesus said, 'When two or three are gathered together in my name, then I am in the midst of them.'

When the person starts sharing their problem, listen to them with your full attention taking note, not only of the words they are saying, but the way they speak them, the hidden messages of confidence or inferiority, anger or fear, that are conveyed through their body language, the way they project themselves through their clothes, hairstyle, bodily posture, eye contact. I do not mean the kind of analysis a psychologist might make, just the kind of instant impressions we all have of someone when we meet them. If anything they say, or anything about them, seems to hold your attention particularly, silently turn to

Jesus and ask Him if it means anything. It may be that you get a fleeting idea come to your mind. It may be just a simple word like 'fear'. Give this back to Jesus and ask Him to clarify it and give you wisdom to know what to say or pray.

An elderly lady once responded to a word of knowledge about fear of water.

All the time she spoke to us she kept her head down and fidgeted with her necklace. I thought, this woman looks more guilty than afraid. I thought I was just trying to be clever but prayed about it just in case. The impression grew stronger and eventually I asked her gently if there was anything she felt particularly guilty about. Suddenly an intense shuddering seized her and she confessed how many years ago, when in a state of deep depression, she had tried to drown her baby.

As Marilyn and I prayed, the Holy Spirit came, releasing and healing her. Some three years later an elegantly dressed lady came to say thank you at the end of a concert. We didn't recognise her at first then as she reminded us, I could only stare in amazement. Totally gone was that face-hiding posture. She was holding herself proudly erect, smilingly looking at us in the eye.

Do not Judge

I have found that it is vitally important to keep giving back to God everything we notice or wonder about, and not just go barging in with our impressions. Just the other month a lady came for prayer to be filled with the Holy Spirit. As I looked at her I saw she was wearing more make-up than the average woman and wondered if she was using it as a mask to hide some deep hurt. Sure that I was right, and not bothering to check with the Lord, I rushed into this new subject, telling her God wanted to heal her heart and enable her to trust again. She looked at me, totally puzzled.

'But I haven't got any deep hurts or heartbreak,' she said, 'I had lovely parents, I'm doing well in my job and I've got a smashing husband and kids. I just wanted to move out more in the gifts!'

We live in a very judgmental society and sometimes it is hard to distinguish between our instinctive cultural reaction and God's reaction. The Pharisees had this problem. They were the religious authorities, the ones who were meant to really be in tune with God's ways. Yet when they found an adulterous woman, all they could think about was judging her, whereas Jesus wanted to forgive her. Even His friends jumped to the wrong conclusions and tried to hustle the little children, or the immoral people, away so that He could get on with the important things.

No one understood that Jesus wanted to bring emotional as well as physical healing to the woman who reached out to Him in the street. They were shocked when He, who with one breath spoke healing and forgiveness to those broken by sin, in the next lashed out with a white, searing anger at the hard-hearted hypocrisy of the Pharisees. When Jesus was here in the flesh the disciples were stumbling behind Him, never fully hearing and understanding. After He had ascended and the Holy Spirit came, the ability to hear God and understand Him, to move in His timing and His ways, to flow with His compassion and to judge with His judgments was born within them. This is hugely encouraging, because it was when they were in the same boat as us, without the physical presence of Jesus but filled with the Holy Spirit that they truly heard Jesus and did the things He did. Thus Peter, when he met the crippled beggar at the gate Beautiful, didn't give him money as he certainly would have done in the past, but listened to Jesus and gave him healing. In the same way, when Ananias and his wife tried to deceive the apostles with the amount of money they were offering, the apostles 'heard' the Lord, knew what was happening and responded with that same righteous judgment that Jesus had displayed.

What About Evangelism?

The same principle of listening to God should apply in our efforts to evangelise. Church after church organises big evangelistic programmes, invites famous evangelists to hold rallies and crusades, and encourages their congregations to witness in the streets. All these things are good and necessary, and often bring about wonderful results, but what often seems to be missing is teaching on hearing God's whisper to go to this or that person as He leads. Many Christians who are by nature quiet and shy feel terrified at the thought of having to take part in some massive event or to look conspicuous in the streets. They then feel ashamed and worthless compared to those who are more exuberant by nature, and say that they don't have the gift of evangelism. Well, it is true that we are not all evangelists, any more than we are all teachers, but I believe that if we were taught more to expect God to speak to us, giving us a little nudge to go and speak or pray for someone, or a deep burden of compassion for someone in need, or a word of knowledge that we can share with them, then the power and love of God could be more released to the sort of people we are rubbing shoulders with all the time.

I remember one night when I first knew Marilyn, there came a knock at her door. Just as I was opening it the phone rang and Marilyn answered it. The man on the doorstep explained that he had fitted double glazing at the back of the house and wondered if Marilyn wanted the rest of the house fitted too. As Marilyn was still on the phone I invited him in. I felt a bit awkward as we sat looking at each other and was just about to offer him a drink when the thought came into my mind 'Tell him about me!'

I can't do that, he's just a salesman, I don't know him, I panicked.

'Tell him about me.'

'Um, did you know that Marilyn is a gospel singer?' I blurted out, blushing furiously.

He leant forward, 'No, that's interesting, I knew she was a musician but not the gospel bit, what's that mean then?'

I fumbled something out about singing songs about the love of Jesus and the new life and hope Jesus brought to people.

'Does Jesus really do that, I thought He was just history?' He paused. 'You know, I had a car crash three years ago and was badly injured. Thought I'd lost everything. That's why I couldn't finish her windows. I'm just getting myself together again now but my confidence is all gone. Do you think your Jesus can do anything for me?'

Just then, Marilyn put the phone down and came into the room. The man introduced himself and they started to talk windows. They said two sentences and the phone rang again so while Marilyn answered it, we went back to talking about the Lord.

In all, the phone rang about eight times that night. Marilyn never got to discuss the windows, but by the time he'd left I'd told him all I could think of about the Lord and he was still asking. He didn't become a Christian there and then and as I've never seen him since, I've no idea if he ever did. But what I do know is that God directed me and enabled me to hold that conversation and when he left he had a new look of hope in his eyes.

Divine Encounters

While it is true that Jesus often talked to thousands at a time, yet there were numerous occasions too when He had what we might call 'divine encounters' with people. For example, when

He was sitting casually by a well one day, He had a word of knowledge for a woman that led, not only to her becoming a Christian, but also to many others from her community. When passing along a road surrounded by crowds of people, He suddenly knew that high over His head in the branches of a tree was a man called Zacchaeus. This man was hated and feared by the Jews because of the extortion he practised and Jesus, using the wisdom only God could have given Him, invited Himself to Zacchaeus' home. Zacchaeus was so touched by the love of God that his whole lifestyle was transformed and he wanted to give money away rather than extort it. Nathaniel and Nicodemus both became believers after Jesus spoke to them individually with words that were divinely inspired.

After Jesus ascended and the Holy Spirit was poured out at Pentecost, there are further stories of the disciples being led to witness in this same way. Peter was led by an amazing vision to go and speak to a Roman Centurion and his family and Philip was led by both an angel and the Holy Spirit to speak to an important Ethiopian official in the desert.

There are other biblical examples, but the exciting thing is that people today are still experiencing the Lord leading them to individuals often with dramatic results. In his book, *Power Evangelism*, John Wimber tells how he was flying one day. As he glanced across the aisle at his fellow passengers, he was startled to suddenly see the word 'adultery' as if written across a middle-aged, business man's face. In the next instant a woman's name came to mind. Startled, but sure from the peaceful knowing in his heart that this was the Lord, John leant forward and quietly asked the man if the name 'Jane' meant anything to him. The man went white and asked if they could talk somewhere. They went up to the little bar and on the way the Lord also said to John, 'Tell him if he doesn't turn from his adultery, I'm going to take him!'

When the man demanded who had told John he replied, 'God

did!' and went on to give him God's warning. Instead of an angry outburst as John expected, the man broke down and prayed the most heartfelt prayer of repentance John had ever heard. After further discussion he went and confessed to his wife who was sitting next to him on the plane, and she too became a Christian.[1]

It is true that John Wimber is a well-known speaker but he is still an ordinary man! It is so easy to think, 'well that will happen to someone like him, but not to me'. But it is nothing to do with how famous we are but how much we are ready to listen and respond to God! I was once attending a church lunch and was getting really bored! I couldn't hear any of the chit-chat going on all round me and so I just went off into a day dream. I suddenly became aware that specific thoughts kept going round and round in my mind and they seemed to be for the woman next to me. I hadn't even looked at her but I gave her a quick glance now! Again the thought came to me, 'This woman has a problem with a man (I felt I knew specifically what the problem was). If only she will put her trust in me and in my love for her, then this problem would take its proper place in her life.'

My heart was thumping and my hands were sweating. The least thing I wanted to do was talk to this woman. I wouldn't even be able to hear her and suppose it was wrong? I prayed the Lord would take the thought away if I was being deceived or make it stronger if it was from Him. Much to my dismay it got stronger. Eventually I plucked up the courage and asked her if she would pop outside with me for a quick word.

When I told her what I believed the Lord had shown me she burst into tears!

'How did you know?' she wept.

'It was the Lord, by His Holy Spirit,' I answered gently. 'He showed me because He loves you so much and knew how you were being pulled apart.'

'But I don't understand! How could the Lord know this about me? How can you say He loves me? What does it all mean?'

I was amazed. I had been thinking all this time that she was a Christian, after all it was a church lunch! But as we got talking it became clear that she knew nothing about God and had only come on the off chance that morning because of seeing the notice about Marilyn singing there. I was able to tell her all about Jesus and how she could know His love and healing in her life. She kept saying, 'I can't believe God can know the very details of my life like that. It must have been meant that I came and then sat next to you today!'

At the end of this conversation this dear lady, who had known nothing about Christ, decided that she wanted to become a Christian herself and made an appointment with the vicar to follow that decision through.

He Knows the Right Time

You see, the Lord loves this world so much and longs for each person to come to know Him. But because He is the One who made us, He alone knows what will get through to us. That is why listening to Him is so important. I believe that many people come to a point where they are ready to believe in God, there is a hunger in their hearts to know the truth that has often been brought about by some crisis. It is at that point that the Lord, responding to their unconscious prayer, might put a little idea in our mind to speak to them, or give us a burden to pray or to help them in some practical way.

Jennifer Rees Larcombe tells in her book *No Hands but Ours* how she felt a deep burden for a lady in her road. For a long time all she could do was pray for her as she resisted all Jen's efforts to be friendly. But one day she broke her leg and needed help. For several weeks Jen looked after her and one day Diane said she wanted to go to church with Jen. Soon after that she became a Christian. God knew that it wasn't crusade type preaching that would bring her to Him, but prayer and love.

We are not all crusade speakers or people with up-front ministries but we are all channels of God's love to the people He has given us. We have all been given the mind of Christ and the Holy Spirit as our counsellor. We have all been given spiritual gifts and ministries suitable to our calling and character. As we listen to Him and follow His guidance and strategies and allow His love to mould our reactions and judgments, it may well be that the person who hears God and offers to do the shopping and cleaning for a frail old lady, or who speaks a word of kindness to a harassed shop assistant, will have as powerful an effect as the one who has been called to preach from a platform.

9
Hearing God in Today's World

A Spiritual Battle

Some years ago, Marilyn and I were taking part in two evangelistic meetings following a conference.

On the first evening we went to the hall with a great deal of anticipation but there were less than twenty people there and they sat in a stony silence all evening.

The next morning, Marion, one of the conference leaders, talked to us.

'I feel the Lord's been speaking to me about last night,' she said. 'I have a strong feeling that we should be praying more specifically over the actual site. So today we are going to pray inside the hall and also march round it, claiming it for God.'

When we did this, an amazing thing happened. We stood in the hall silently waiting on the Lord and suddenly people began to share impressions that God had given them. As they spoke, a coherent picture emerged, that at some stage in this hall's history, satanic, ritualistic meetings had been held. We thought at first that was everything we needed to know, but it was after a young girl had a vision that we began to see clearly what we were praying about. As part of the witchcraft rituals, a baby had been sacrificed to Satan.

Horrified by this revelation and shaken by its implications, we asked God how we should pray about this. Again one person after another had ideas which came together as a whole plan of prayer.

Together, with one voice, we were to come against the evil powers that had held this building and site for so long. We were to destroy their hold and claim back the building for God. Together, we were to imaginatively place the baby into the Lord's hands and pronounce His forgiveness over the people who had carried out the evil deed. The Lord showed us that by following these steps, the atmosphere and the very fabric of the building could be cleansed and healed. We continued speaking out the name of Jesus and His light, joy, love and freedom into every corner, until we all felt a deep sense of peace.

Later that night, every seat was full and there were still people coming in. They were crowded at the back and even sitting on the edge of the stage! God poured out His Spirit that night. The people not only laughed at the jokes and listened attentively. They responded in their hearts and when the appeal was given at the end crowds of them came forward, even some children as young as four. One man felt it wasn't for him, left to go home and returned twenty minutes later saying, 'I couldn't go in my front door until I'd come back and put myself right with God.'

Listening for the Roots

In Chapter 4, I talked about how we can hear God through the created world and the everyday things around us. In this chapter I want to go a step further. That as we listen for God's voice within the places and events in which we live, we can begin to sense something beyond the mere circumstances and beyond even a personal word that God might want to give us. We can begin to sense something of the spiritual powers and battles that are operating behind the scenes, to come in tune with what God might be saying or doing in a certain area or through a certain series of events. We can learn to pray or act according to His heart and purposes and so help to advance His kingdom. This is what happened at that evangelism conference. There were invisible evil powers at work in the very building, which had been made strong and powerful because of the human sacrifice. That is why on the first night's meeting even though the Word of God was preached and a great deal of prayer had been put into it, there was no response.

None of us could have known that this had taken place. But God knew! When Moses asked God, 'What shall I tell them your name is?' (Exod. 3:13 [paraphrase mine]), God answered, 'I AM WHO I AM' (v.14). Similarly, Jesus answered those who were querying His authority, with the incredible statement, 'before Abraham was, I am'. God knew what had happened, not just with a vague sense of looking back into a distant memory, but because He is always in the present, seeing it happening there and then. As we listened to God, He revealed these things to us. When we then prayed the way He directed us, His kingdom was advanced, first in an invisible way in the transformed atmosphere of the building and then with transformed lives.

Discerning of Spirits

In 1 Corinthians 12:7–11, Paul lists the spiritual gifts that we can receive from the Holy Spirit. One of these is the 'discerning' or 'distinguishing of spirits'. This is the ability to see beyond the merely external appearance of something to the underlying spiritual forces.

When I try to understand what this means, it helps me to think of Marilyn and my other blind friends. Marilyn can never, as most of us do, rely on what she sees in a person's face to know what they are feeling, but often when I am convinced that someone is happy, Marilyn will sense their underlying sadness.

My eyes have shown me the external reality but Marilyn has discovered the true reality.

In the same way when we look or listen to the things around us, our senses may show us the external reality: this is a beautiful area; this town seems rather desolate with so many shops closed down; this is a strange series of events etc. But as we talk to God and ask the Holy Spirit to give us discerning hearts, we may, like Marilyn, discover more of an underlying spiritual reality. 'So we fix our eyes not on what is seen, but what is unseen. For what is seen is temporary, but what is unseen is eternal' (2 Cor. 4:18).

What was Behind the Problems?

There was once a time in our ministry when everything seemed to go wrong. The recession hit us and we did not have enough money to pay the bills. Several members of the team decided to leave and we couldn't find anyone to replace them. All the requests for bookings dried up and Marilyn became ill and uncharacteristically depressed. Was it time for the Ministries to close down? Marilyn had always prayed that God would provide both the finances and the bookings for as long as it was right for her to be ministering in this way. Could this then be a sign that He was bringing it to an end? But no, deep in her spirit, she did not feel this was the answer, she knew that God's call to minister through song had not changed, so why wasn't He answering our desperate prayers for provision when He always had before?

One day, when returning from a concert, Marilyn was crying out to God about the situation when He began to speak to her. It was as if she suddenly 'knew' that a certain group of people were praying against her and the ministry. As she continued to listen to the Lord He showed her that she needed to pray for herself, for her house and for the Ministries office which had all been curse targets of this group. Before going to bed that night she prayed in the way she felt God had shown her. Immediately, she sensed the terrible depression lifting and a deep joy began to bubble up from within. From the next day onwards people began to send in anonymous gifts, some for incredible amounts. The following month was transformed from being one of our slackest ever to our busiest month that year!

In Ephesians 6 Paul warns us to be aware of the true nature of the battle we are in:

> Finally, be strong in the Lord and in His mighty power. Put on the full armour of God so that you can take your stand against the devil's schemes. For our struggle is not against flesh and blood, but against the rulers, against the authorities, against the powers of this dark world and against the spiritual forces of evil in the heavenly realms. (Eph. 6:10–12)

In that crisis situation in the Ministries, we thought we were fighting against things like the recession, illness, a waning of interest in our ministry. These were all elements of what was happening, but they were not the cause. It was only as Marilyn sought the Lord with all her heart that the root cause began to be revealed. The devil is described as the 'deceiver' and 'father of lies'. We were being deceived into thinking that the ministry should be ending but the devil was using the things like the recession and lack of bookings as the tools to carry out his curses. As soon as Marilyn obeyed the way she felt the Lord was leading her to pray, all the 'natural' causes lifted!

Just a Place?

As I've meditated on this and similar situations and as I've listened to teaching at church and studied the Bible myself, I've become aware that both sin and godliness can in a definite way affect the atmosphere of a place or even an object. A building may look like a simple structure of bricks and cement; a town may appear to be just the usual conglomeration of houses, shops, offices and busy people, but it's the quality of its spiritual life that God sees most of all.

It is recorded that while Jesus 'healed all the sick and demon possessed that came to Him', in his own hometown 'He could not do any miracles there except lay hands on a few sick people and heal them and He was amazed at their lack of faith.' So the unbelief and refusal of the people in that town to acknowledge that He was God affected the atmosphere of the whole town.

Conversely, the family at Bethany, Mary, Martha and Lazarus, warmly welcomed Jesus into their midst. Here was one of the only places where Jesus could truly relax with people, knowing that there weren't any ulterior motives or secret plans to trap Him. There He was loved and worshipped and the place became special to Jesus, a place where He returned again and again. It is hardly surprising therefore that this is the place where Jesus did the outstanding miracle of raising Lazarus from the dead.

Floyd McClung, author of *Living on the Devil's Doorstep* writes about Amsterdam where he had been ministering for several years as a leader of a YWAM team:

> I am convinced that Amsterdam is a city under spiritual bondage. Years of submission to liberality and experimentation, through sexual immorality have opened it up to demonic forces that control many lives . . . Man's sin and rebellion here have opened up doorways through which Satan has been able to enter many hearts, sinking his talons into the life of a whole city.[1]

It is easy when faced by such blatant evil to react in the only way that seems possible as Christians, to judge and avoid it.

One of Floyd's team was one day overwhelmed by some of the aggressive and sexual sins he had witnessed. He found himself wondering:

'If all this is acceptable, then what on earth goes on behind closed doors?' In his heart he sensed God answering him:

'If only you had to witness some of the things I see, you would know how grieved I really am.'

God was grieved, but He still loved the people and Floyd and team, sensing the heart of God, did not react in judgment and avoidance but in daily prayer and intercession around the city, breaking the demonic bondages and claiming it for God. Floyd comments:

'We are certain that such slow and deliberate prayer was essential to all that has happened since.'[2]

Sodom and Gomorrah

As I read the Bible I found that the saga of Sodom and Gomorrah especially reveals our need to listen to what God shows us about an area rather than just go by our senses.

Physically, Sodom was a beautiful place: 'Lot looked up and saw that the whole plain of the Jordan was well watered, like the garden of the Lord . . . So Lot chose for himself the whole plain of the Jordan . . . Lot lived among the cities of the plain and pitched his tents near Sodom' (Gen. 13:10–12).

To Lot's eyes the fact that it was a beautiful and fruitful land meant that it was good. He had eyes only for the surface reality and had no understanding of the evil forces lurking behind the loveliness. Abraham, however, made his choice solely on the basis of what he had heard from the Lord. 'The Lord had said to Abram, "Leave your country, your people and your father's household and go to the land *I will show you*"' (Gen. 12:1 [my italics]). 'Abram lived in the land of Canaan' (Gen. 13:12).

Although Abram, like Lot, had gazed upon the beauty of Sodom, he was so in tune with God that he was able to hear the whisper from God's heart telling him what it was really like, 'Then the Lord said, "The outcry against Sodom and Gomorrah is so great and their sin so grievous that I will go down and see if what they have done is as bad as the outcry that has reached me . . ."' (Gen. 18:20–1).

The way that God expressed Himself to Abraham was interesting. He said, 'The *outcry* against Sodom and Gomorrah is so great and their sin so grievous . . .' (my italics).

The sinfulness of the two towns had become an 'outcry' to God. What was a beautiful, fruitful land to Lot was a screaming, distorted uproar to God.

Similarly in Isaiah 65 and other similar passages God shows that the nation's sin is a tangible reality to Him. 'Such people are smoke in my nostrils, a fire that keeps burning all day' (Isa. 65:5).

The Generational Effect

The two books of Kings describe the ongoing tragedy of places becoming tainted with the effects of man's sin from one generation to another. Israel was meant to be the holy nation, yet became defiled by the people turning to false gods and indulging in evil practices. As one leader succeeded another the level of evil and wickedness intensified. Like our experience with the village hall, the nation, despite all the prayers of the righteous and the declarations of the prophets, remained in bondage to sin. Even when the rare godly leader emerged, they still did not heed the God-given directive that the evil of the nations contained within the places and things that had been used for the purpose of that evil, needed to be destroyed. 'In the second year of Jehoash . . . Amaziah son of Joash king of Judah began to reign . . . He did what was right in the eyes of the Lord . . . The high places, however, were not removed; the people continued to offer sacrifices and burn incense there' (2 Kings 14:1–4).

Not Just Curses but Blessings

Some of these examples may seem to be rather negative, referring as they do to possible holds of the devil. But in the same way, the blessing and peace of God can be imparted into our environment.

I remember on one occasion going to the park for a walk with Marilyn and a friend who had come to visit us for the day. After strolling around for quite a while we decided to sit down on a sunny patch of grass near the main path and have a little time of praying for each other. People were wandering past and suddenly an amazing thought came to my mind. I knew from the deep sense of peace and awe within me, that this was a thought from God. This is what He told me:

> 'You are just praying for yourselves, but because you love me and have welcomed my Spirit amongst you, this little bit of ground has become a holy, sacred place. Because of that, these passers-by are being touched by my love, even though they don't know me and you are not praying for them.'

We were all amazed by this thought. If we, by our few moments of prayer, had enabled the holiness and love of God to touch a little bit of parkland and the unknowing passers-by, how much more could an area or building that was consistently bathed in believing prayer, touch the atmosphere and the people with God's Holy Spirit?

I remembered some of the churches or Christian conference centres I had been in where the sense of God's peace seemed almost tangible, and the difference just a few miles could make when one area was highly influenced by materialistic and achievement values, the other by the local Christian community.

Vibes or the Holy Spirit?

People often say things like 'Oh the vibes were good in that place, that's why we bought it . . .' or 'You could just tell something had happened there, it had such a sad atmosphere . . .'

When non-Christians hear these kinds of statements, they presume that the person has had some kind of psychic or telepathic experience. But what I am talking about is not telepathy or extra-sensory perception. It is not looking to the things and places themselves to communicate some out-of-this-world knowledge, but to the Almighty God, the One who is omniscient – all knowing, and omnipresent – everywhere at once. It is having the understanding that God is the One who is sustaining this world and working in all places, and in all things, and in all people, and is bringing all things to their ultimate conclusion. That is why it is so important to be listening to Him, not just in different places but in some of the things that happen in our world today.

Listening to God in World Events

When Hitler started to pass laws against the Jews in the early 1930s, most governments and countries considered it merely a German problem. Even after Hitler had crossed the Rhine, and taken Austria and Czechoslovakia, people still refused to listen to what was really happening. It was like the prophecy of Isaiah being fulfilled, '[You will] be ever hearing, but never understanding; [you will] be ever seeing, but never perceiving' (Isa. 6:9).

In her book, *Listening*, Anne Long writes:

> I have discovered two ways of listening to the news. One is to 'just listen' to what is happening in the nation and world,

> aware of what is going on yet detached, letting it go in one ear and out the other. I may hear the facts but not their significance. The other way is to listen Christianly, to begin to hear from God's viewpoint and listen with His ears.[3]

I read this book for the first time shortly before that tragic murder in 1993 where a toddler, Jamie Bulger, was abducted and killed by two young boys. The injuries and nature of his death were horrific and the whole nation was shaken by it. This came after a whole series of violent crimes and I'd been aware in my own heart of a kind of blasé attitude as I read about each one.

On this occasion, having started to put Anne Long's teaching into practice, I asked God to show me His heart about this murder. As I turned to the reports a deep grief began to well up within me. My hard-hearted, cynical attitude melted away as I began to sob. It was as if I could suddenly see, not just the agony of the little boy's final moments, not just his parents' devastation, but the blackness of fear and frustration, of hopelessness and abandonment that was in the hearts of the children who had killed him.

Even as I sobbed I understood more. That it was not even simply the sin of those two boys, but the sin of the whole nation. The hopeless degrading social conditions, the lack of moral teaching in schools and homes, the violent videos and films, the tendency in all our hearts to hurt and destroy.

I knew this grief was not my own. I am too hard and judgmental to feel so deeply. It was God weeping through me in the same way that He wept over Jerusalem. It was God transforming my own response of hatred and rejection to Jesus' own prayer: 'Father forgive them, they know not what they do.'

What is the World Coming to?

Last week I was waiting for the bus home after a shopping trip. Some elderly ladies were chatting together and I heard some fragments of their conversation:

'I don't know, it seems no one's safe nowadays. Can't even go out the door without wondering if you're going to be attacked.'

'Yes, it's terrible int'it? We're not even safe in our own homes. And no one's got any respect any more, especially children. Now when I was a child . . .'

'And that MP who was accused . . .'

'Oh they all get in bed with each other nowadays. Got no moral values any more. Look at those girls having babies at fourteen. Don't know what the world's coming to . . .'

A phrase in that conversation really stuck in my mind as I got on the bus:

'I don't know what the world's coming to . . .'

When we read the papers and hear the news, or experience the evils of society in the lives of our own family or friends, most of us withdraw in bewilderment. Our instinctive trust in the world around us and in the culture which has framed and developed us, is being threatened and eroded. We are made fearful and insecure and instinctively push the whole worrying problem away with the dismissive, 'Don't know what the world's coming to . . .'

But the thought that kept niggling me as I sat on that bus, is that we who are Christians *do* know what the world is coming to. God has told us in His Word what the ultimate destiny of this world is to be. He has also spelled out that there will be certain signs and characteristics that will mark what the world will be like in its last days. I thought again about that conversation I had just heard. The ladies bemoaning the lack of respect, the moral decline, the darkness and fear outside their doors . . . and a verse I had read recently began to take on a new significance. As soon as I got home I looked it up.

> There will be terrible times in the last days. People will be lovers of themselves, lovers of money, boastful, proud, abusive, disobedient to their parents, ungrateful, unholy, without love, unforgiving, slanderous, without self-control, brutal . . . treacherous, rash, conceited, lovers of pleasure rather than lovers of God – having a form of godliness but denying its power. (2 Tim. 3:1–5)

I sat with the Bible in my hands reading this verse over and over again. There in a passage penned 2000 years ago was the same picture of society that those ladies had been describing today. It was as if the writer was standing in one of our High Streets looking about him and planning an editorial for the daily paper!

I had read this passage many times before, sometimes even in concerts, but this time one particular phrase seemed to stand out to me: 'There will be terrible times *in the last days*' (my italics).

I suddenly began to understand that what those ladies had been describing, and what I and many other people often passed off as 'just life nowadays', was actually one of the means by which we could interpret the signs of our times. God was saying in this passage that in the last days before His return and final judgment, society would become dark and self-centred, violent and godless. Of course, people have been like this all through the ages, but it seemed to be indicating that in an unprecedented way, the whole of society would be affected.

Suppose, I thought to myself, just suppose this passage is referring to *this* society, *this* time that I live in now? Suppose it is not simply that certain aspects of our society happen to fit this picture, but that it is actually an indication that Jesus' return is imminent? What should I be doing? How should I be praying? What should I be expecting? How can I truly recognise what God is doing?

I got up and started pacing around the room praying out my thoughts to God. I stopped by the window and looked out. The scene was normal and peaceful. Small white-washed houses across the road, children playing outside. Our big blue van parked safely in the drive, cars going by . . . everything so normal and typical. What was I doing worrying about the state of the world and whether those last days were really now? Of course they weren't! There's probably hundreds of years to go yet, I thought, and sitting down comfortably firmly pushed the thoughts away.

It was the next day, just as I'd crossed a busy road, that God suddenly put a question into my mind: 'If I was to return tomorrow would you be ready?'

I stopped in my tracks. 'No!' was my immediate response. I knew I was not ready.

'Would the world be ready?'

Again, I thought 'No!' Instantly, yesterday's images that I'd been trying to push away, rushed back. In my mind's eye I could 'see' the present suffering of this world: Romania; Rwanda; the former Yugoslavia; the evil tyrannies and resulting devastation of whole societies; the starvation and homelessness of millions of refugees and children in the Third World countries. The thirst for power; the nuclear battle and threat; the earthquakes and famines; the racial hatred; the growing level of marriage breakdown; violence, drug usage, sexual abuse, suicide, mental illness, murder; the moral sleaziness; cynicism and despair . . .

'Lord,' I whispered, 'so much of the world needs you, please send your Holy Spirit that people might know you. Only you can show them the truth of your love. Only you can pierce through that darkness and bring people into the light. Please fill us with your love that people can be reached and made ready before the end.'

I will pour out my Spirit

As soon as I stopped running away from my disturbing thoughts and faced the true picture of our society, my prayer became 'Please send your Holy Spirit.' I recognised that in order to deal with the unprecedented level of darkness in the last days, there would need to be a parallel, sovereign move of the Holy Spirit.

In the last chapter I quoted the prophecy from Joel 'And afterwards I will pour out my Spirit on all people . . .' (Joel 2:28).

Like the verses in Timothy about the state of society, Joel is talking about the last days before Jesus comes again to claim His own and to establish His eternal reign. Joel is saying that there will be an extraordinary outpouring of the Holy Spirit on all people in those days. A greater outpouring than ever before. That everyone, even the most ordinary and weak in our societies will be filled with the Holy Spirit and have the capacity to receive supernatural revelations.

The Toronto Blessing

At the beginning of 1994 a little church in Toronto, Canada, began to experience the blessing of God in a new way. Hundreds were meeting with God in a dynamic experience that continued occurring over weeks and months. Physical manifestations such as falling to the ground under the power of the Holy Spirit, shaking, laughing and weeping became common as the Lord sovereignly melted away demonic bondages and natural holds of fear, unbelief and spirtual dryness. But for most people the most wonderful effects of this outpouring were not the physical, but the spiritual. A deep hunger for God was being born in people's hearts. A love for Him and for His Word; the joy of love and obedience replacing the dryness of tradition; a renewed vision and understanding of what Jesus had done for them; a new compassion and longing to reach out to the world.

As the news spread, more and more people began to visit this church. Many came in scepticism about this new phenomenon, ready to criticise and denounce it, only to find they were being bathed and empowered by the Holy Spirit themselves. Early on, people became aware of a remarkable aspect to this renewal. That as God met with them they were somehow impacted with that same power and anointing. When they returned to their own fellowships they then found that the Holy Spirit began to flow through them, meeting with and empowering people there in the same way. At the time of writing, this has now been going on for over eighteen months and what has been referred to by Christians and secular media alike as the 'Toronto Blessing' has become a world-wide blessing and outpouring and it is still growing and spreading.

What is Happening?

Increasingly, over this past year I have found myself praying 'What is happening, Lord what are you doing?' On the one hand there is the growing darkness in society, on the other this rapturous experience of God. Could it be that this 'Toronto Blessing' is the outpouring prophesied by Joel? If so, how should I be responding?

As I have prayed, I have sensed more than ever before the need to be listening to God, to be hearing with the discernment that comes from His Spirit to mine, what He is saying and doing in this day. It is so easy to either smugly dismiss something or to become so taken up with it that everything boils down to 'my experience'.

A Reaching out to the World

The more I've prayed the more I've understood that God is pouring out His Spirit in His intense longing for the world to come to know Him and to be made ready for His return. The darker the world grows the more God's heart is broken. He hates sin and evil but He loves people with a love that we cannot even begin to comprehend. It is often the awareness of that love of the Father God that has so overwhelmed people in this new outpouring. God does not want to meet anyone as Judge, but longs for us all to know Him as Saviour and Friend on the day of His return. 'The Lord is not slow in keeping His promise, as some understand slowness. He is patient with you, not wanting anyone to perish, but everyone to come to repentence' (2 Pet. 3:9).

The wonderful thing is that when people take time to really seek Him and intercede, to listen to God through His gifts of knowledge and discernment and reach out to the needy and sick in the power of God's Spirit, the kingdom of God is inevitably advanced into the world. The way Jesus used a word of knowledge one day is an example. A woman came up to draw water while Jesus was sitting at a well. Jesus opened up a conversation with her during the course of which He almost casually mentioned that He knew that she had had five husbands and was living with a man who wasn't her husband.

The impact of this simple word of knowledge was far reaching. As Jesus put the spotlight first on her inner emptiness and thirst then on her married state, her life turned around. Knowing that she was loved even while known, she opened up to Him to the extent that she was the first person to hear directly that Jesus was the Messiah!

As I read this story I was amazed afresh at its modern feel. This woman of 2000 years ago was experiencing the same brokenness of her life and hopes that so many face today.

Cynicism is a hallmark of our society. We have grown to expect that if we don't or can't look out for ourselves then no one else will. Love, for many, has become a cheap term for sex and those who hope for better things are dismissed as idealists. All these things this woman was experiencing, but through the supernatural intervention of God, her life was transformed. Having been scorned and despised in her own village she now ran back full of conviction and boldness. She became a witness to the very people who had rejected her and openly declared that Jesus 'told me everything I ever did'.

She invited them to come and see for themselves and the final outcome was that 'Many of the Samaritans from that town believed in Him because of the woman's testimony . . . they urged Him to stay with them, and He stayed two days. And because of His words many more became believers' (John 4:39–41).

When people are confronted by something that could only have been revealed by God, the defences are crumbled and the power of God is released sometimes resulting, as in this story, with whole communities meeting with God.

In his book, *Does God Speak Today?*, David Pytches tells the story of a miracle that took place in drought-ridden Guatemala in 1965. The whole city, Santa Rosa, was in a state of crisis with animals dying, crops failing and businesses failing. All the churches were holding daily prayer meetings but there was no reprieve until one day a message in tongues was given at a small Pentecostal gathering. When the interpretation was brought it said simply 'Dig a well in the pastor's backyard. There you will find water.'

This word caused instant controversy and derision. Why the pastor? Why that Fellowship? The work began and showed no result. People lost heart as they tackled the rock hard ground with no sign of water. Some dropped out but the core group, believing the word, battled on. Finally after six days of solid digging, they managed to remove a huge boulder and as they did so a gush of water was released!

David writes:

> It was a remarkable sign for the whole town. What the miracle of the well did for the growth of this church carries on until this day. The number of conversions to Christ was staggering, the entire town was influenced by it. Church membership grew from a few dozen to over nine hundred within that same year.[4]

The Power of God and the Devil's Counterfeits

It is this kind of supernatural intervention of God's power that will enable us to truly fulfil Jesus' commission to reach the ends of the earth with the gospel. In the last days, it is not the time for one or two new members to be added to the Church each year, but for whole communities to be reached for God. But just as there were those who tried to copy the miracles or use the power of God for their own evil purposes, Jesus predicted that in the last days there would be great deception and confusion. He warned us to be on our guard against false prophets and teachings:

> Watch out that no one deceives you. For many will come in my name claiming "I am the Christ" and will deceive many . . . do not believe it. For false Christs and false prophets will appear and perform great signs and miracles to deceive even the elect if that were possible. (Matt. 24:4–5, 23–4)

At this present time there are more of these false and deceiving elements in our societies than ever before. In the last two decades alone, the West seems to have opened its arms to the East, and having rejected the traditional image of Christianity, has turned to the mystic teachings of the Gurus, the yogis and Islam. It is now accepted, and often medically advocated, that Yoga, transcendental meditation and alternative remedies such as acupuncture and hypnotism are a normal and healthy part of our society. A couple of months ago Marilyn watched a TV chatshow where a witch was interviewed and was chatting about how beneficial she, and her coven's spells, are to individuals and therefore to society. Just last month I read how Satanic groups are lobbying for equal recognition as churches.

The Cosmic Picture

Immediately following Jesus' prophecies about the devil's counterfeits in the last days He goes on to say 'Nation will rise against nation, and kingdom against kingdom. There will be famines and earthquakes in various places. All these are the beginning of birth-pains' (Matt. 24:7–8).

Every time I read those verses I find myself praying. So many nations and kingdoms have been at war in the last few years that people have felt overwhelmed at each new report of some fresh, devastating crisis. Millions have perished in famine conditions. Earthquakes have hit with tragic results in Japan, the USA, Greece etc.

Lord, what are you telling me?

I am not attempting to analyse or assimilate the details of all these things. I don't know enough for that, in fact, I probably know a lot less than most people because I do not hear the news and conversations, and church teaching tends to pass over my head! But I have still become aware over the last couple of years how important it is to be ready. When I started studying the different verses to do with the end times that I needed for this chapter, I was interested to see just how frequently the theme kept coming up: watch and be ready, watch in this case being synonymous with 'listen', 'take in', 'be alert', etc.

> No-one knows about that day or hour, not even the angels in heaven, nor the Son, but only the Father. Be on guard! Be alert! . . . Therefore keep watch because you do not know when the owner of the house will come back . . . If he comes suddenly do not let him find you sleeping. What I say to you, I say to everyone: "Watch!"(Mark 13:32–7)

About six years ago Marilyn and I were staying with a lovely Christian couple. Over tea one night they started to tell us of a baptism they had attended recently. The baby being baptised was about nine months old and was babbling happily in the vicar's arms as he prayed for her. He prayed a long prayer, asking the Lord to bless her and bring her to Him, for her to serve God and find His plans for her life. For her to marry the man God had in mind for her . . .

Suddenly, there was an interruption. The baby sat bolt upright in the vicar's arms, looked down the length of the church and said in a loud voice that everyone could hear, 'There won't be time for all that to take place before the Lord Jesus returns!'

We were stunned by this story. How could a baby who could not even talk, say such a thing? It was impossible!

Well, we still don't know to this day if that really did happen or if it was just a dramatic story. We have no way of proving it, but what we do know is that couple believed it. They were just an ordinary, straightforward man and woman but they were convinced of what they had seen and heard. As we reflected more we realised that what is impossible with man can always be possible with God. After all, if He spoke to Balaam through a donkey and to Moses through a bush, could He not also speak through a baby?

To me, the significance of that story was not so much that a baby spoke prophetically or even that we could guess at the time of the Lord's return. That would be falling into the trap of many of the cults anyway, because Jesus Himself said, 'No one knows about that day or hour, not even the angels in heaven, nor the Son, but only the Father' (Matt. 24:36).

To me, the significance again seemed to be that God wants us to be ready and expectant, listening, watching and ready for our Lord's return.

A Beautiful Bride

Last year, some dear friends of mine, Judith and Cefyn, got married. When I saw Judith on the days leading up to the wedding she was full of joyful anticipation. I was close enough to see her face as she walked down the aisle and she looked radiant. It wasn't just the beautiful dress or the lovely hair and make-up, it was the inner knowing that was shining out from her that soon she would be joined to the man she loved. They had both been waiting and preparing for that moment and now it was to be fulfilled.

As I've prayed and tried to listen to the Lord's heart in these times I live in, there are still many things I do not know. What is happening in our society seems in many ways to fit the biblical picture of the world in the last days. But that does not mean that we *are* in those days for sure. The Toronto Blessing could be the beginning of that final outpouring, but we don't know that for certain.

Close to Him

But what I do know is that God wants me to be alert, listening and responding to Him. As each new development occurs to bring it to Him and ask what He thinks about it. He wants me to read the newspapers with His Word beside me. To walk the streets or pass through different experiences with the Holy Spirit at my side. To ask Him to change my judgmental, or cynical, or apathetic responses into His responses of love and forgiveness. To be working with Him towards His goals being fulfilled: for the world to be reached, not just saved but made whole. Finally, not to be sleepy or complacent like the five virgins or household servants that Jesus told about, but like my friend Judith, to be radiantly ready to meet Jesus, my bridegroom.

'Let us rejoice and be glad and give Him glory! For the wedding of the Lord has come, and His bride has made herself ready' (Rev. 19:7).

PART 4

Becoming one with Him

10
Handling our Mistakes

'It must be wonderful always knowing what God wants you to do!' Sharon said wistfully.

I smiled ruefully thinking of the many hours of anguish it had taken me to make some decisions recently.

It is easy for us to feel that other people will be so in tune with God, that they will always be right, where we will almost certainly be wrong! We attribute to others a spiritual wisdom and authority, forgetting that in Christ we are all equal and, therefore, all have the same potential, both to hear God and to make mistakes!

Mistakes! We all dread making a mistake when we are trying to hear God. Many of us refrain from stepping out in the spiritual gifts altogether because we feel so afraid we'll get it wrong. On the other hand, we can become so self-confident that we give up checking out our desires and decisions against God's Word.

The Right and the Wrong Voices

Just as I started writing this chapter my friend Julia arrived. She had volunteered to do some gardening for us which we were thrilled about. When I popped out to see how she was doing I was amazed at the transformation. Already half of the front border was clear of weeds and the shrubs looked neat and pretty instead of like a jungle.

To me, at a casual glance, weeds and the plants seem quite

similar. Both have roots, stems, green foliage and flowers. Both, if left untended would grow and spread. Yet where the flowers and shrubs create a beautiful garden, the weeds are ugly and potentially harmful.

That's what this business of hearing God is like, I suddenly thought. There are so many other 'voices' that could be speaking to us. Our own ideas and judgments, our desires and hidden motives, even the devil who is constantly at work to tempt us and lead us astray, yet disguises himself as an angel of light. How can we be sure that what we are hearing is God's voice when they all seem so similar? And even if we are sure it is God, have we heard fully what He wants us to know or are we acting on half knowledge? Have we failed to receive His wisdom to know what to do with our knowledge . . . ?

Revealing the Roots

Watching Julia as she carefully dug beneath each root, I saw that they are the key to both gardening and listening to God. The true 'flowers' of God's words will have good roots (in the Bible) that bring about a perfect beauty and order, while the 'weeds' will have bad roots (in our own desires or the devil's temptations) which in the long run will bring about disorder and damage. Maybe each time we have an impression that we feel is from God, or if we've shared something or acted on something that we mistakenly thought was God, we need to look and see what its roots reveal to us.

Pride

I remember the time I had a 'prophecy' in a concert which became a very long and involved saga about the last days. It fell completely flat and afterwards I lost all sense of the presence of God with me. In the end I knew I had to talk to God about it.

'Lord, please show me what happened, what did I do wrong?' I prayed.

As I sat silent before Him, I realised that I had given the prophecy, not because I had been truly seeking to understand God's heart, but because I knew someone in the audience and wanted to impress them with my spirituality by bringing a dramatic 'word'. At 'roots' level it was my pride speaking, not the voice of God.

I was shocked to see this truth about myself but I have found that it is something that can happen again and again, often without us even being aware of it! There can be a subtle attraction in giving words of knowledge and prophecies. To know something that no one else knows, to have the power to be 'God' to the 'lesser' people around you who aren't so spiritual as you! To have the authority to advise someone what to do while hiding under the cover of it being a 'word from God'. All these motives can be lurking undetected in our hearts. I wondered if it was this kind of thing that was behind this tragic story I heard of a short time ago.

A young woman was at a meeting and at the end went forward to receive some prayer ministry. To her amazement, the counsellor began to pin-point some things that had happened in her life that she thought no one knew about. This man is a true prophet, she thought, and listened to him with close attention.

At some point she mentioned that she was engaged and would soon be getting married. At this, he said, 'I believe the Lord is saying that this man you are marrying is not the right one for you. If you are obedient to the Lord and give this man up before you have committed yourself to him, then in a year's time you will marry the man that God has chosen to be your husband.'

She was shaken and confused by this revelation. Would God really tell her to give her fiancé up? But this man was a prophet, he must be right. After all God had shown him things about her that no one else knew!

At great cost and heartbreak she broke off the engagement. Each time the sadness and regret threatened to overwhelm her she tried to comfort herself with the reminder that in just a few months she would marry the right man. As the months went by she began to get worried. She hadn't even met anyone yet! She started looking at each man she met with new eyes, wondering if he was to be the husband God had chosen for her. A year came and went, no man, no husband. Eighteen months, two years, nothing.

Devastated and broken she is now receiving counselling.

The prophet in this story was on the right track for as long as he brought the words of knowledge which were truly from God. Maybe when he saw her awe and incredulity as each detail was revealed, he was tempted to bring what he thought was a word of direction from the Lord.

There is a verse in 1 Corinthians that says very succinctly 'Knowledge puffs up but love builds up' (1 Cor. 8:1).

If he had been truly motivated by the love of God, he would have realised the devastating effect such a 'word' could have on her and the danger of telling someone something that was so extremely directional and limiting in its time span. I believe that if God truly wanted someone not to marry, or to take a certain course of action, He would show them themselves rather than through someone else. Or if He did speak prophetically, it would be to confirm something that the person had already begun to sense.

Our need for wisdom

Sometimes our belief that God has shown us something can so excite us that we forget to ask God for His wisdom to know what to say. I fell into this trap once with devastating results.

During the concert I had a growing sense that God wanted to speak encouragement to a woman who was having trouble conceiving. As I prayed about this I seemed to suddenly 'see' that her problem was emotional not physical and had its roots in something her mother had done to her when she was tiny. I felt excited by this, thinking that it could be a real breakthrough for the woman. If she could be emotionally healed then maybe she would have her baby. Without stopping to think, I jumped to my feet and shared this 'word' exactly as it came to me.

When the concert was over a small group of ladies came up looking distressed.

'We think your word was for our friend . . .'

I was about to say, 'Oh that's good, do you want me to pray for her?' when they continued.

'She'd never had any idea her mother might have done such a thing to her. She's gone home very upset. What shall we do?'

I was stunned! Not until that moment had I realised how devastating such a word could be, not just for the person it was intended for, but for everyone there who was having trouble conceiving. The more I thought about it, the more I felt sick. The nature of the word was such that there was no way the person could check it out and so put her heart at rest. Unless the Lord gave her supernatural peace she could be forever suspecting her mother.

Somehow I managed to pray with them for their friend, but that night as I tossed and turned, the Lord spoke into my heart: 'Why didn't you wait until you knew what I wanted you to do? Why didn't you check it out with me and seek my wisdom first? Why did you put giving a word before giving my love?'

Two days later I received a letter from the pastor saying that while they had been very blessed by the concert as a whole, he was concerned by the word and the number of people that had been upset. He pointed out that as the church was just beginning to move out into the spiritual gifts, many people had been frightened away.

Grieved and saddened I wrote to the pastor, confessing I had been wrong to bring such a word and asking him to pass on to the people concerned how very sorry I was to have caused such hurt. The pastor wrote back very lovingly expressing his forgiveness and releasing me from the guilt of what had happened. He also expressed his continued support for us as a team which deeply touched me.

Directed by His Love

My wrong handling of my word made a lasting impression on me and from then on I determined that with God's help I would never again put the excitement of having a 'word' before knowing His wisdom and communicating His love. Some verses in 1 Corinthians confirmed to me one day just how important this is.

> If I speak in the tongues of men and of angels, but have not love, I am only a resounding gong or a clanging cymbal. If I have the gift of prophecy and can fathom all mysteries and all knowledge and if I have a faith that can move mountains, but have not love, I am nothing. (1 Cor. 13:1–2)

In his book *Does God Speak Today?* David Pytches tells the story of a couple who had a child who was born seriously disabled with cystic fibrosis. A doctor told them that there was a 'one in four' chance that any other children they had would also be affected.

They had just become reconciled to the fact that they would only have one child when someone in their church 'prophesied' over them that they would have a normal child. On the basis of this 'word' the wife joyfully conceived again, but when the baby was born it was even more disabled that the first one.[1]

God's Grief

These mistakes happen again and again. Each time I hear another example or fall into the same trap myself, I feel shocked and saddened. How can something that is such a beautiful gift from God be so misused? As I've prayed, I've began to sense God's own 'heart' grief. He has given us these gifts in order that we might know and speak His heart of love into the needs around us. God's thoughts and ways are so much higher than our own and our own hearts can deceive us. We may think we know God's very best for someone and pray/prophesy accordingly, but it must be God's all seeing, all powerful love that fills, controls and speaks through us. In most of these stories a strong desire to bless and encourage their friends has been present, but interpreting these desires as the definite word of God for them creates a false spiritual authority that can have devastating results.

Weighing up Prophecy

There have, of course, been occasions when God really has inspired such words and the results have been wonderful. I believe that the important thing is to give each impression that we feel may be a prophetic word back to the Lord, together with our own desires for the person and not do anything until we know God has given us confirmation that it is from Him. This is what Paul means when he talks about weighing up prophecy: 'Two or three prophets should speak, and the others should weigh carefully what is said' (1 Cor. 14:29).

I personally find that it is helpful to tell someone else, usually Marilyn, before I share anything that is very directional. Many times Marilyn has enabled me to see the need for caution in how I share something, whereas I am often too caught up in it to take that kind of objective stand. If she feels herself that it is from God it gives me extra confidence to share it with God's authority.

What is our Foundation?

Much more serious are the mistakes we can make when we subconsciously put our own desires and values before the Word of God.

A young man wrote to us to say that he and his girlfriend had got engaged but that in the meantime, because of their circumstances, they were living together as man and wife. This was sad enough, but sadder still was his comment that as they had prayed God had shown them this was the right thing to do. He had no idea how much he had been deceived by his own desires but if only he had kept his roots based on what the Bible said, he would not have been able to make such a tragic mistake.

God is Merciful

We will make these mistakes, probably over and over again, but what I find so incredible is that God is a lot more patient with us than we are with ourselves. He is our Father and just as a human father takes the time to teach his son to walk so God is patient and loving as He teaches us to listen.

What He wants from us is not so much a constant perfect performance, but the heart desire to seek Him and know Him. It is our heart that He looks at, rather than the outward appearance. 'The Lord does not look at the things man looks at. Man looks at the outward appearance, but the Lord looks at the heart' (1 Sam. 16:7).

If our hearts are intent on knowing and loving the Lord, then even if we make mistakes, God will turn them to the good in our lives. I found this to be true in a wonderful way, several years ago.

In July 1985 I came to the end of my BA degree. I was relieved that I had got a good grade but was worried about what I should do with my life. One day during my quiet time a little verse seemed to take on tremendous significance. It was as if I had underlined it with a fluorescent pen! 'Lead out those who have eyes but are blind, who have ears but are deaf' (Isa. 43:8).

As the verse mentioned the blind and deaf I decided that was to be my career focus. I applied for all kinds of jobs and courses. One opened up, to become a technical officer for the blind. I was accepted for a course to start the following April, all I needed was some experience and I quickly sorted that out by becoming a volunteer helper at a local blind school for girls.

I had only been at the school a fortnight when the headmistress called me into her office and told me she didn't want me to carry on.

'It's too much of a risk with your hearing problems, and to be honest I think you're going after the wrong career,' she said.

I was devastated. I'd been so sure this was God's guidance but I'd got it totally wrong. What was I going to do now?

Before I left the school a blind lady, Penny Cooze, came in one evening to speak at the Christian Fellowship. We got chatting and it was Penny who asked me that momentous question with which I opened the Prologue: 'Would you like to meet Marilyn Baker?' What happened next you already know!

I'd mistaken the true meaning of that verse in Isaiah and run for the wrong thing. But because God knew I wanted to do His will, He used my mistake to lead me to the right place. The interesting thing is that in all the years I've known Penny, she has only ever been to that school once to speak, and that was during the fortnight I was there. God's timing was perfect!

Getting the Balance

We meet people who refuse to believe that God will speak in any other way than what He has already made known through the Bible, and others who talk at length about the constant new words and pictures God has given them.

We can become so intense about being led by the Spirit that every minute detail of our lives has to be guided by Him. This can be taken to absurd lengths, as shown by a story in Joyce Huggett's book, *Listening to God* where a woman would not put on any article of clothing until the 'still small voice' gave her permission![2]

It is not that the Holy Spirit will never guide us about that kind of everyday decision. There have been several occasions, for example, when I have had a sense that a particular concert outfit will be right and have been amazed at how well the colours have gone with the background. There was even a time when I was in despair with my hair! I tried to style it but each time it looked a total mess. One night it was causing the usual problems and I sent up an urgent prayer, not at all expecting any answer. I was astonished when a very clear and specific thought came to my mind: 'Put it on the side!' My hair parts naturally in the middle so I nearly pushed the thought away thinking I was mad. I decided on the spur of the moment to try it out. After all, I had nothing to lose! It came out beautifully and I've worn it on the side ever since!

It is when we base everything on what we feel God has shown us, that we make mistakes. I sometimes feel, 'Goodness these people are so spiritual, I could never hear God like that!' But when we question some of them more closely, we see that they are relying on their revelations more than the Bible and sometimes even abandoning the Bible altogether! We may think 'What does that matter? I know the Bible so well already, what's important now is to have a real, present communication with God, not something that was written thousands of years ago!'

Well, Jesus warned us specifically not to be deceived by groups or individuals claiming to have fresh revelations about God. Today the number of fringe Christian groups, cults and heresies is accelerating dramatically. Many of these groups have originally started off as an authentic part of the Church and then a powerful individual within the group has taken one particular aspect of Christian doctrine or phrasing and magnified it out of all proportion. Soon, what has been just one aspect becomes many, for as even the smallest child knows, one lie leads to another. This is what happened in humankind's very first experience of temptation when the devil threw doubts into Eve's mind about the authenticity of God's Word. While this tragedy opens in Genesis, the Bible closes on the same note with the solemn warning:

> I warn everyone who hears the words of the prophecy of this book: If anyone adds anything to them, God will add to him the plagues described in this book. And if anyone takes words away . . . God will take away from him his share in the tree of life and in the holy city. (Rev. 22:18–19)

Jesus shows us the way

When Jesus was attacked in the wilderness it was with that same subtle temptation, to follow His own desires, to doubt the Word of God and to make God's Word say something it doesn't. Jesus did not discuss these issues with Satan, or try to rationalise how they could be right for Him. He just answered each statement with the simple words, 'It is written . . .' God's Word was His foundation stone and nothing could make Him swerve from it.

Our Response

A Prayer

Lord Jesus. Thank you that love for your Father was what constantly motivated you. You loved and knew the Word of God and it was the foundation of all you thought, said and did. Thank you that in all your daily decisions you listened ceaselessly to your Father and followed His strategies as you carried them out.

Lord you know that I have made many mistakes and am often led by my desires rather than by your Holy Spirit. Please forgive me, Lord. Please take my mistakes and use them to help me grow more like you. Please set my feet on the foundation of your Word and give me such a longing for your truth in my life that the devil will not be able to make me swerve from it. Thank you, Jesus. Amen.

11
Time to Listen

Recently I got into a bad argument. Unable to resolve the issues, I threw on my jacket, slammed the door behind me and walked agitatedly to the park.

I came to the waterfall and sat beside it. I gazed mesmerised into the flowing waters while my emotions continued to battle within me. But all of a sudden, I became aware that Jesus was with me. I wasn't praying, yet somehow I knew He was there. I found my thoughts being drawn away from myself and onto Him. The peace of the surroundings also began to penetrate my consciousness and melt away the heat of the argument.

There were little sticks and debris flowing with the water over the fall. But I noticed that where the stream narrowed down a few feet away, some of this debris was unable to get through and as more and more pieces flowed down it was beginning to form a little dam. As I watched it was as if Jesus seemed to whisper in my heart: 'Don't let the memory of this argument become like that dam. Don't block my Spirit by holding on to your anger. Let my Spirit of love flow through you in a cleansing stream and take the bitterness and hard words with Him.'

There and then I lifted up the 'dam' of my anger and hurt to Jesus and asked Him to cleanse me. Over the next hour I sensed Him bathing me, loving me, forgiving me and giving me the power to forgive. I talked to Him about some recent difficulties and perplexities and felt the comfort of His peace. As darkness drew in I moved to quietly loving and worshipping Him. By the time I returned home a longing had been born within me to know Him in a much deeper way than ever before.

Our Hunger for God

Many of us come to that point of becoming aware of our hunger for more of God. It is the same longing that the Psalmist expresses so beautifully and poignantly in Psalm 84. 'How lovely is your dwelling-place, O Lord Almighty! My soul yearns, even faints, for the courts of the Lord; my heart and my flesh cry out for the living God' (Ps. 84:1–2).

But how do we put that longing into practice? Most of us live such busy, frantic lives, always aware of something else that needs doing, someone else we need to see. There seems so little time for deep intense periods of listening to God. Even if we suddenly find we have got more free time than usual we can fear giving it to God. Maybe deep down we think we should be using the time in a better, more productive way than just praying.

This was just the position Martha found herself in one day. Jesus and His friends had suddenly turned up needing tea and a bed for the night and Martha felt overwhelmed as she tried to think of everything at once. At least she had enough food in the house, but it needed so much preparation. After all, it was Jesus! Carrying yet another dish into the dining room, Martha was incensed to see her sister Mary doing nothing but sitting on the floor, so close to Jesus she was almost perched on His feet. And oh dear, she had that old sloppy expression on her face as she looked up at Him! Martha felt her own face redden with embarrassment. What must Jesus think of her? Surely the girl should know by now that a woman's place is in the home! Without stopping to think, she marched into the room and interrupting Jesus in the middle of His sentence, blurted out, 'Lord, don't you care that Mary has left me to do all the work by myself? Tell her to help me!'

She was stopped as Jesus gently shook His head, 'Martha, Martha . . . you are worried and upset about many things.' He glanced down at Mary's upturned face then turned back to Martha, 'only one thing is needed. Mary has chosen what is better . . .' (Luke 10:38–41).

By temperament I am much more of a Martha than a Mary! I love the Lord so much and yet I can spend hours flitting around doing things like cleaning, ironing, worrying about things that need to be done etc.

Sometimes I read inspiring books like Joyce Huggett's *Listening to God* or Richard Foster's *Prayer* and think, 'Oh dear, these people have gone so far ahead in the adventure of prayer and listening to God, how can I even be thinking of writing a book on the subject?'

And yet I've gradually come to understand that listening to God and being willing to take time out for God are not things I should do in a competitive spirit like getting enough grades for a degree! Instead, God wants me to come to Him because I truly want to. It is my heart He longs for and it is when I become willing to lay down the things that I consider important and acknowledge that there may be only 'one thing [that] is needed', that I find within me a longing and hunger for Him that a quick prayer could never satisfy.

Little Lay-bys

Marilyn and I were recently given a copy of Joyce Huggett's book, *Finding God in the Fast Lane* (see endnotes). Both of us found it revolutionised our prayer lives and in fact we ended up buying it for most of our friends for Christmas! Joyce expresses such pearls of wisdom, and I would recommend it to anyone seeking to go deeper with God in the midst of our busy lives.

At the time, Marilyn and I were extremely busy with concerts and I was still wondering how to give more time to God on a regular basis.

Joyce suggests using little lay-bys in the midst of our day to turn our hearts and minds to God in worship and love. Moments like our bath times; when we are stuck in rush hour traffic; when we're sitting down with a coffee before starting the day's chores; when we have our lunch hour at work; all can become Him-centred rather than self-centred. Some of us may feel 'but I just don't *have* any moments like that in my day' or 'I live with non-Christians and it would upset them!' But if we love someone we still make that time for them, even if we've got 'no time'! Joyce gave the example of a woman whose husband became violent whenever she prayed, so she started closing her eyes during the TV adverts. Her husband thought she was just having a little nap, but she was using those few minutes to come close to her Father.

Being Mindful

Joyce often talked about 'mindfulness' saying that even in the midst of what we are doing, we can keep our hearts and minds on Him in loving attentiveness and thankfulness. I began to try to cultivate a thankfulness to God for the small things around me. The opening petals of a flower; an open fire on a frosty day; the sharp summer tang of raspberries and blackberries with ice-cream. A father tenderly lifting his little daughter on his knee for a cuddle and the peaceful expression on a child's face as he falls asleep. I tried to stop and look at them with new eyes and new senses. To see the love and character of God being expressed through them and let my heart respond in praise and love to Him.

This took time and practice to develop, but I began to find an amazing thing happening. That the more I focused on God in these small everyday details the more my love for Him grew and deepened. I found too that my awareness of the times when He wanted to speak to me prophetically through everyday things was heightened as I learned to love Him and thank Him in this ongoing 'mindful' way. Also I was becoming conscious of Him giving me little ideas or hunches about things, maybe to write to somebody or go and visit someone. This had happened before but I had often pushed away the thought thinking I was daydreaming. Now I am finding more and more that God really does give me fleeting ideas in this way. This kind of intuitive awareness is what Joyce was saying we need to develop in our relationship with the Lord. That if He wants to speak to us, or draw our attention to something we will be ready and waiting for Him.

Taking Time Out

Many of us go to church week in, week out. While there we may sing choruses expressing our ability to nestle in God's love, things like: 'How precious O Lord is your unfailing love, we find refuge in the shadow of your wing. We feast Lord Jesus on the abundance of your house and drink from your river of delight' or 'You are my hiding place . . .'

But in reality, all these songs are expressing something that takes longer to achieve than a quick communication from God while we are rushing around in our day or even while we are at church. How often do we really take that time to 'feast', 'find refuge', 'drink' or 'hide' in Him? To do this requires a conscious decision to switch off to the outside world and run into His arms!

There comes a point when we need to make more time for Him alone. More time even than when we just stop for a few moments to tune in to Him. We need time to withdraw for an actual period from the busyness of our lives, in order to renew our inner resources.

In 1995, Marilyn recorded a song that really expresses this need. It is called 'I Take Time':

I take time to be quiet with Jesus.
He stills my heart with His gentle love.
I feel the joy of His full acceptance,
His mercy streams from His throne above[1]

If there has been a storm at sea, then even when the wind drops, the waves still carry on surging. Gradually the stillness of the atmosphere will affect the momentum of the waters until they in turn become still.

When we are living at our normal jet-set pace our thoughts, emotions, spiritual and physical responses are often surging and storming. Even when a crisis or particularly hectic day has passed we can still feel tense and hassled. Just as the sea needs that drawn-out exposure to the calm skies, so we at times need that more drawn-out exposure to the Lord so that He can 'still our hearts', give us new joy, and cover us with His 'streams of mercy'.

Thomas Merton talks about this: 'If we really want prayer we'll have to give it time. We must slow down to a human tempo . . . The reason why we don't take time is a feeling that we have to keep moving. This is a real sickness . . .'[2]

Cancelled Engagements

When Marilyn was at the Royal College of Music she heard a sermon one day about us needing to be willing to follow God's plans. 'If we truly want God to be Lord,' the speaker emphasised, 'we need to be willing to cut out the things that are superfluous in our everyday lives so that we have more time for the important things.' The message went home and that night Marilyn decided to pray about the forthcoming week.

'Lord, you know I've made many plans, but I want you to be

in charge of my week. Please put a stop to anything you know is not the very best for me.'

One by one, as the days went by, her plans were cancelled. Friends rang to say they were sick, had double-booked, had to go away etc. Eventually it came to the weekend. She was sure this would still hold. After all, she was going to be fellowshipping with Christians and there couldn't be anything better than that! Early on Saturday morning her friend rang to cancel because the family had chicken pox.

Fed up and bored, Marilyn went upstairs to her room. Lying on her bed she picked up a Braille magazine at random and started to read. To her shock, she found herself reading a poem expressing how we can spend so much time rushing around doing things, even praying and having fellowship with Christians, yet never spending intimate times of love with God. Marilyn suddenly saw that God had not cancelled her plans because He was trying to spoil her fun, but because, in His love for her, He wanted some time with her Himself. There and then she asked Him to forgive her for putting 'things' before Him. As she opened herself up to Him, His gentle Spirit met with her, bathing away the tensions of the week, refreshing her heart, revealing deep and beautiful insights to her spirit and mind. At the end of that weekend she felt so happy, as if she had been with the most dear and stimulating of friends, yet humanly she had been alone.

Joyce Huggett writes:

> We who sometimes sacrifice so much by living in the fast lane need to recognise that there are times to drive with the foot hard on the accelerator, times to pull into life's lay-bys and times to stop and seek real refreshment – from stillness and worship, meditation and fellowship.[3]

About two years ago Marilyn and I were doing a concert for a beautiful Christian community in Worcestershire. We had been extremely busy and were both feeling tired and spiritually dried out. The morning after the concert the director and his family came to pray and bless us before we went home. Touched by their loving acceptance, Marilyn began to share how stressed she was feeling. After praying together Roy expressed a thought that was truly full of the Lord's wisdom.

'You're giving too much time to the problems and not enough time to God to show you what to do about those problems,' he said. 'Try taking one day each week, not Sundays though, because you usually work then, and use those days as Sabbath days to rest in the presence of Jesus, to receive His love afresh, to listen to His voice and find out His plans.'

How did Jesus Cope with Stress?

This advice went home and the more we thought about it the more we realised just how much of a biblical principle it was. Jesus Himself consciously created times where He could be alone with God His Father. He had as much pressure on Him as any 1990s white-collar commuter! He had His mission to fulfil by a pre-determined time. As the leader of a team He was always needing to make the decisions. He was constantly barraged with vast throngs of people calling for Him to heal them; people talking to Him, demanding answers, trying to catch Him out and betray Him. Add to that the constant spiritual battle against the prince of darkness who was using any, and every, means to destroy Jesus and we'll begin to get a picture of the degree of pressure He was under.

But although Jesus felt everything we might feel, He was never overwhelmed by His feelings. 'What,' I wondered, 'was Jesus' secret? What enabled Him to stay on top?' I believe that it was the times that He built into His schedule to be alone with His Father God that gave Him His tremendous grace, power, love, strength and ability to know what to do in each situation. 'Very early in the morning, while it was still dark, Jesus got up, left the house and went off to a solitary place where He prayed' (Mark 1:35).

We don't know *how* Jesus prayed in that time but it is interesting that at the end of it Jesus obviously sensed a fresh confirmation and anointing on His ministry and had received new understanding and specific direction for that day, 'Jesus replied, "Let us go somewhere else – to the nearby villages – so I can preach there also. That is why I have come"' (Mark 1:38).

A few months ago I was attending a 'Listening to God' day at the Pilgrim Hall Conference Centre in Essex and Peter Garrett, the Director, told us how he had been in confusion about how the coming year should be planned out. In the end he decided to spend a day alone with God, seeking Him for wisdom and guidance. As the hours passed by, God met with Peter and step-by-step revealed His plans for that year and as Peter listened and obeyed all the confusions melted away.

Our Sabbath Days

From my journal:

> Woke up with a feeling of strangeness . . . today is different. We're not doing a concert so what is it? I go downstairs and put the kettle on. I see the post has arrived and pick up the bundle of letters and start slitting them open in preparation for reading to Marilyn. But suddenly I remember, I can't do that today! Today we're letting things like the post and the cleaning rest. We've put today aside to be a day for the Lord!

On this first day we both felt very uncertain about how to use the time wisely. We were so used to rushing around doing things. How should we start? We had Joyce's books but we didn't just want to follow a list of someone else's suggestions, we wanted to meet with God for ourselves. But could we really pray for a whole day?

In the end the time flew by! We did many different things, some together and some quietly on our own with God. We each had an extended quiet time, really taking time to study and drink in God's Word and talk to Him about what we were reading. I found that when I gave Him the space to talk to me, new insights and understandings of His heart were suddenly filling my mind. It seemed as if Jesus were close beside me, revealing His heart to me, speaking deep within my spirit His words of affirming love. As I drank in the things I felt He was saying to me I moved instinctively into worship. Normally I find this very hard when on my own and my worship tends to be hollow and self-conscious. On this day I just felt that I wanted to express love to Him. I started thanking Him for all the things He was showing me and for His love and friendship. In moments my prayers became much more focused on Him, rather than on my needs. Soon I found I was praying and praising Him in tongues and I experienced a deep joy welling up from within me as God brought to my mind truths that usually I was so familiar with they had failed to mean anything.

We experimented with being silent before Him and at the other extreme with conversational prayer with the two of us and Him together. We made our lunch time a special occasion, remembering those beautiful verses from Revelation 3, 'Behold, I stand at the door and knock. If anyone hears and listens to and heeds my voice and opens the door, I will come in to him and eat with him and he shall eat with me' (Rev. 3:20 [Amplified Version]).

So we made lunch as if for a special friend, using nice china and glasses as well as creating a lovely meal. We tried to have things that reflected the incredible variety and beauty of His creation. Instead of grace being a quick muttered prayer at the beginning of the meal, it became the centre-piece of the whole meal, as we took time to focus on the lovely things he'd made and brought Him into our conversation.

That afternoon we went for a prayer-walk in our lovely local park. We strolled along the paths watching the children playing, enjoying the fragrant flowers and the gentle breeze, listening to the trickling waters of the streams and canals, feeling the sun warm on our faces and the short grass prickly against our legs. When we sat down for a rest, we were drawn again into worship and thanksgiving. We started to pray and this time consciously asked God what He wanted us to pray for and how, instead of just picking out any need that came to mind. As we followed His directions we had an awe-inspiring sense that we were truly in partnership with the Almighty God.

God met with us that day. As soon as we gave Him the time and space to speak to us, He came close to us. At the end of the day we both felt refreshed, not just physically but spiritually, mentally and emotionally too. We didn't have any incredible revelations about our work, we weren't sent off on any amazing faith exploits. But what we did find was that a greater hunger had been created within us to come closer to God, to hear His voice, to be in tune with the gentle nudgings of His Holy Spirit.

And after . . .

Like most of us, we have not always succeeded in continuing to give God this time aside. Roy had suggested one day each week and we tried that for a few weeks, each time experiencing the closeness and love of God in a new way. After that we got very busy with concerts again and it was hard to get into a regular pattern. But we have found that each time we do take time out, even if it is only a couple of hours rather than a full day, we find that our spiritual ears are opened to hear new and deeper things, our hearts are melted and filled with His love, our prayers are enriched and empowered and our spirits are awakened and refreshed. Marilyn has had ideas for songs come to her in the stillness and I have been inspired to write poems or creatively express something He has been showing me.

An Extended Retreat

In January 1995 we went on the two-week retreat with Joyce Huggett (referred to earlier in the book). There we spent each day with God and, under Joyce's gentle direction, learnt to bring our deepest fears and negative attitudes into the light of God's love and Word. Joyce did not pray or minister at great length with us, she just pointed us to God, encouraging us to have an honest 'Deep-calls-to-deep' encounter with Him, holding back nothing of ourselves and pushing away nothing of Him. When we came home, we knew that the way we had met with Him had been real and life-changing. We are still enjoying the benefits of changed hearts and attitudes today.

OVER TO YOU

1 Find a time when you can be quiet with God and put it into your diary! It doesn't have to be a full day, in fact if this is the very first time you've tried taking time out for God it may be best to keep it short at first then gradually build up. It could be a period of one to two hours.
2 Find a place where you can be alone and undisturbed. Jesus pointed out our need for this in true prayer. He said, 'But when you pray, go into your room, close the door and pray to your Father, who is unseen. Then your Father, who sees what is done in secret, will reward you' (Matt. 6:6). This could be your bedroom or any place in your house where you feel you can be private and comfortable. If you are worried about the phone take it off the hook for a bit! If you wanted to, you could go for a walk. Moses, Elijah and Jesus all heard God in a special way when they were on a mountain top. Not many of us live near mountains but there may be lovely parks, gardens, fields or beaches nearby.
3 From a purely practical point of view, I find that if I want this time with God first thing in the morning, it is best to actually

get up, wash, dress, and have breakfast before I start. There've been plenty of times when I've woken up, thought blearily 'This morning's free, could spend some time with God.' Prayed for five minutes then gone to sleep again! Sometimes it can be helpful to fast, especially if we are seeking God for a particular thing. But on the other hand, if fasting makes you feel physically ill or distracted by thoughts of food, then it may be wiser to eat so that we can relax before Him.

4 Don't rush into reading the Bible or praying! First invite the Holy Spirit to come and spend this time with you. It says in Psalm 37:7, 'Be still before the Lord and wait patiently for Him' and in Psalm 46:18, 'Be still and know that I am God.' Being still, giving our eyes time to see, our ears time to hear, our minds time to assimilate, our spirits time to bathe and our bodies time to relax in the knowledge that our loving Heavenly Father is with us.

It might help to look at something that could bring you into a place of stillness. The scenery, if you are outside, or a vase of flowers. A simple cross or a meaningful picture or object. When I was in Cyprus, Joyce Huggett had a beautiful carving on her table. It was a single piece of wood carved in such a way that it looked like a man's figure reaching down and tenderly holding the upstretched hands of a little child. I have never been one to get much out of things like pictures and statues, but as I looked at this, it seemed to touch something deep inside me. All I could think of was the tenderness of God's love for me and somehow looking at that carving brought me into the place where I was able to receive that tender love for myself.

5 While becoming still, you may be aware of agitated thoughts, anxieties and tension battling within you. Don't try to fight them away. Instead, thank God that He knows about these things and gently, but consciously, release them into His hands. Jim Borst writes:

> We become alert and attentive. Not with a violent effort but by letting go of all tensions, excitement, anxiety, worries . . . While all these flow out of us there remains only one thing: attention to the Lord, awareness of the presence of Him who is the author and giver of all peace and strength.[4]

6 Read a Psalm or a devotional passage/poem. Use it to continue to focus on God's love, His character and His ways. Start to thank Him for the things you are reading about Him. Move on from there to looking about you in an attitude of thankfulness. Be attentive to His loving hand as you look, listen, touch and smell. Keep bringing any areas of need in your life to Him, as they occur to you and ask Him to talk to you about them as you are meditating. If you can, start to worship Him – you could try singing some uplifting choruses or singing in tongues.

7 Ask God to speak to you through His Word. Read a Bible passage slowly and meditatively, asking Him to reveal to you new insights about Himself and anything that needs transforming or healing in your own life. This is how this writer reads the Bible at a time like this:

> Read quietly, slowly, word for word, to enter the subject more with the heart than with the mind. From time to time make short pauses to allow these truths time to flow through all the recesses of the soul. During these peaceful pauses the Holy Spirit engraves and imprints these Heavenly truths on the heart . . . [abbreviated][5]

8 Have a time of intercession and ask Him who He wants you to pray for. If someone comes to mind talk to Him again and ask Him how to pray. Keep on praying until you have covered everything He has shown you.

9 Ask Him if there is anything He wants you to do, or anyone He wants you to see – if an idea comes to mind talk to Him about it and ask Him for the confirmation of His peace. Ask Him for wisdom to know when and how – and then do it!!

10 If any thought or idea comes to you that does not make immediate sense, write it down. Pray it back to Him and ask Him to fulfil it in His time and way, then leave it in His hands.

11 Continue with your normal routine but try to maintain that awareness of Him with you. As you cook, thank Him that His creative love is flowing through your hands into the meal. As you deal with people at work thank Him that He, the One who is full of 'grace and truth' is speaking through you.

12
If You Love Me You Will Obey

A Command to Give

We had taken a three-month sabbatical but when we returned to work we found that our finances were £7000 in the red. The bank gave us a week to repay the overdraft or our account would be closed and the Ministries would have to shut down. We had no idea what to do. It was too late to advertise for people to covenant to us and we couldn't take out another loan. All we could do was pray! We were going away the next day, so before we went we met together and prayed very simply that God would provide us with the necessary £7000 by the following week. When we returned it was the day before the deadline and we all felt nervous. Our administrator, Trudy, rang us that night in great excitement. '£5,500 has come in,' she said. We were thrilled but also a bit sad as we had asked for the full amount. Still maybe the banks would accept this for now. The next day Trudy rang again. '£1,500 came in this morning,' she told us.

Later we saw some of the letters that had come with the money gifts, many of them expressing things like: 'We had a sudden burden for you all and we felt God wanted us to send you this money to help you in your work.'

The gifts ranged from 50p sent by a little girl, to £1,000 from a business man. As each person obeyed their individual prompting from God, the exact amount we had prayed for was sent to us.

On this occasion and in many similar stories, incredible things have come about as ordinary people have heard God's voice and responded in faith to what they have felt God was showing them. These people were in tune with God in such a way that when He spoke they *knew* that they needed to obey, even though they didn't always understand why.

It was this 'in-tuneness' with God's voice that led to the following story. It happened to an ordinary girl who was studying at Roffey Place Christian Training Centre in West Sussex.

A Command to go

The persistent thought kept breaking in on Jane's dream: 'Go to Manchester Airport.'

With a sigh of annoyance she opened her eyes and sat up. She was awake now but that thought, 'Go to Manchester Airport', was coming stronger and stronger.

'Is that you, Lord?' she prayed, 'Do you want me to go to Manchester Airport? But why? What to do?'

There was no answer to these questions so just to make sure, she knocked on the door of the girl next door and asked her to pray with her. To her surprise Helen felt the same, so without more ado, she got in her car and drove to Manchester Airport.

When she arrived she still felt at a total loss. She decided to go and sit in the departure lounge and after a while a lady came and sat next to her.

'Isn't it ridiculous the time they get you here for your flights,' she exclaimed, glancing irritably at her watch. 'I've at least another hour to wait. What time is yours due?'

'Er, well, I'm not actually going anywhere,' Jane said.

'Oh, are you meeting somebody then?'

'No, not exactly.'

'Oh!' The lady looked at Jane curiously, then asked point blank, 'Well what *are* you doing here then?'

Jane took a deep breath. 'Well you see, I'm a Christian and I believe God woke me up and told me to come here.'

There was a long silence. 'That's it now, she'll think I'm mad,' Jane thought to herself. Suddenly she became aware that the lady was speaking again.

'Well, who would have thought it . . .' she was saying softly.

'What do you mean?' Jane asked bewildered.

Suddenly the lady began to cry and gradually the whole sad story came out. A serious row with her daughter many years before, years of bitter silence between them, the daughter emigrating in order to put even greater distance between them.

'But I've just had a letter from her for the first time in years,' she said, wiping her eyes. 'She said that she has become a Christian and wants me to forgive her for all that happened. She wants me to go and see her so that we can start again. That's what I'm doing now, but I still feel so full of hurt and bitterness. In a way I do want to start again but I can't seem to just let go of everything like she has.'

'But that is what being a Christian is all about,' said Jane. 'God knows you can't change your own feelings, that's why He died on the cross for us, both to forgive us and to give us the same power to forgive others. If you asked Him He will come to you right now and will heal those painful memories and enable you to forgive your daughter. He could take all that hurt and bitterness away now so that when you arrive at your daughter's you are ready to make that fresh start.'

She listened and seemed to be really drinking it in. Jane continued explaining about God's love and all that the cross meant and the promise of forgiveness and eternal life for all who believe.

'Did you say I could find God now?' the lady asked suddenly.

'Yes,' Jane said. 'All we have to do is open our hearts to Him and He comes to us wherever we are.'

'I want to pray now then,' she declared.

So they prayed together and Jane could tell, even in that instant that something had happened. There was a new look of peace and lightness about her face.

'I feel all kind of relaxed and happy inside,' she said in amazement. She smiled warmly at Jane, 'My daughter won't believe this!' She pulled a sheet of paper from her bag and scribbled on it and then handed it to Jane. 'Here I must rush now, but thank you so much. I know something has changed within me. I know God is with me and I feel different about my daughter now. Here's her address, please get in touch as I will be there for quite a long time.'

She was gone. It was over. As Jane drove back to the college she was full of praise to God that He had used her to lead that woman to Him in such an incredible way.

Some hours later, exhausted, but still full of joy, Jane arrived back at the Centre.

Carrying a coffee, she went into the lounge and switched on the television. Settling herself in front of it, she was startled when the programme suddenly went blank and a newsflash began.

'There has been a serious aircrash,' said the announcer. Jane froze and leant forwards straining to hear. 'A plane crashed on take-off at Manchester Airport. Many have been killed and seriously injured. Those wishing to enquire please ring . . .'

The announcer's voice droned on but Jane sat frozen, then she leapt to her feet, grabbed a pen and scribbled down the phone number and ran into the hall. Five minutes later she returned looking ashen. The lady had been killed.

The one comfort for Jane that morning was the knowledge that the lady had met with God in time. She was not dead but eternally alive with Him. It was with that thought in mind that

Jane sat down and wrote to the lady's daughter to tell her that her mother had become a Christian and had forgiven her just before she got on the plane.[1]

I heard this story for the first time several years ago and am still deeply challenged by it. It would have been so easy for Jane just to have turned over and gone back to sleep. That would have been the most natural and humanly, wise thing to do, after all, she could have gone in the morning! But if she had done that 'natural', 'wise' thing, the lady would have died not knowing God and her daughter would have been permanently saddled with a terrible guilt. God loved that woman enough that He did not want her to die without knowing Him. Maybe He had been seeking someone all night who would be willing to go for Him, after all, Sussex is a long way from Manchester!

To me, the key to all this is that when we seek God and express our longing to hear His voice, we need to understand that what He tells us will always be for a purpose. He never just engages in idle conversation, but speaks to us in order that we might know His strategies or that we might be changed, comforted or used to show somebody else His love. As well as listening therefore, we also need to learn to obey what we hear.

I remember how on one occasion I went to a church with some young people when I was staying in Lancashire. At the end a young man came up and started chatting with them. I asked him his name but it took ages to hear it correctly. I decided after that to keep quiet and let him chat to his friends. Suddenly a very clear and vivid thought came into my mind, 'Ask him what he does as a living.'

I don't want to do that, I thought, pushing the thought away. But it kept pushing into my consciousness each time getting more urgent. In the end I shrugged my shoulders. I had nothing to lose.

As casually as I could I broke into the conversation.

'So what do you do for a living, Robert?' I asked diffidently.

It turned out that he was unemployed at the present time but had worked at a conference centre until recently, doing their sound and recording.

My pulse quickened. We desperately needed a new sound engineer and were faced with an extremely busy schedule without one.

With a sense of excitement, wondering for the first time if this could really be God leading this conversation, I started to ask him appropriate questions. The few I managed to think of to do with sound engineering he answered satisfactorily. Half an hour later I phoned Marilyn. She too questioned Robert on the phone. Two days later he came down for an interview and in another week started work!

Like the Manchester Airport situation, it was just a little thought that in itself did not make sense. I did not know why I should ask Robert his job but it was a growing sense of urgency and rightness that made me go ahead.

If we love Him we will Obey

One day when I was reading in the book of John, I found some verses that seemed to sum up the whole principle of listening and obedience. 'As the Father has loved me, so have I loved you. Now remain in my love. If you obey my commands, you will remain in my love, just as I have obeyed my Father's commands and remain in His love' (John 15:9).

And also, 'If you love me, you will obey what I command' (John 14:15).

In our present society to obey someone seems an old-fashioned concept. People can get quite indignant if they feel they've got to submit to somebody else and any relationship that incorporates obedience is judged as an unnatural evil. Yet as I read these verses I began to realise in a way I never had before, that if I truly loved Jesus then it should be my desire to obey Him. It should be my heart longing to know His thoughts, to hear His voice and to do the things He wants me to do.

'How much do I really love you, Lord Jesus?' I found myself asking one day. 'Am I really in tune with you, or am I only in tune for the things I want to hear, the things that won't cost me?' I sat down on the grass and looked around slowly. Fields stretched away from me in a rolling mass of greens and golds, the leaves of a hedge rustled in the breeze, flowers opened their blossoms to the sky, the insects buzzed and whirred as they went about their business.

The whole of nature is so responsive, I thought. I wish I could be like that. I gazed again at the swaying leaves on the hedge and suddenly found myself praying, 'Lord I want to be like those leaves blowing in the wind. I want to be someone who moves freely and readily at the touch of your Spirit, just as they move freely and readily at the touch of the wind. Help me not to be like one of those branches pinned rigidly to the ground.' As I looked at the motionless twigs I began to remember those times when I had sensed that the Lord was definitely speaking to me, but had been too busy with my own concerns or too self-conscious to acknowledge His voice.

When we Disobey His Voice

One of these occasions was when I was on holiday. The first evening I met a very friendly couple whom I enjoyed getting to know throughout the week. One night I had a dream. It was a very startling, vivid dream in which I seemed to be confronting the wife of this couple about her involvement in witchcraft. In the dream she admitted this was true and agreed to me praying for her release. God delivered her and she prayed with me to become a Christian.

I was amazed by this dream. I had never had such a specifically Christian dream before, nor did I usually remember them. It occurred to me that it may have been God showing me in a dream what He wanted me to do in reality, but I pushed this thought aside. Brenda couldn't possibly be involved in witchcraft, she was just an ordinary woman. It must have just been something I'd been reading. On the last morning, I had about twenty minutes to go before my bus came so I popped in to her room to say goodbye. We were joking about this and that and I mentioned that I'd brought about ten books with me because I was such a bookworm.

'I don't usually bring books but I did this time,' she said. 'A friend of mine has lent me her books on white witchcraft for a bit of fun. It's the good kind so it's all harmless stuff and I'm thinking of getting involved.'

Just then there was a beep outside and I had to go. Never had I been more full of remorse that I did not listen and respond to the Lord's voice when I had the time.

Marilyn was once very busy on a concert tour and suddenly had an urgent impression that she should write to a friend explaining about Jesus. Feeling hassled with all the concerts, and wanting to give proper time and thought to the letter, Marilyn decided to wait until she got back.

When she eventually got down to it all the sense of urgency had faded, but she wrote it anyway and sent it off. A few days later she received a letter returning her own and informing her that the lady had died the week before.

God's Thoughts are Higher

In Isaiah 55 there are some verses which, to me, bring home the whole point of why we should obey God, '"For my thoughts are not your thoughts, neither are your ways my ways," declares the Lord. "As the heavens are higher than the earth, so are my ways higher than your ways and my thoughts than your thoughts"' (Isa. 55:8–9).

If we truly believed in our hearts that God is Almighty then it would be our deep desire to obey His commands, even if we didn't understand them, because we would know that His thoughts and His ways are perfect. Jesus understood this and despite the fact that He, Himself, was God, He was able to say '"For I did not speak of my own accord, but the Father who sent me commanded me what to say and how to say it. I know that His command leads to eternal life. So whatever I say is just what the Father has told me to say"' (John 12:49–50).

So often, like on the above occasions, all I can think of is how embarrassed I will feel, or how unlikely it is to be from God. I look at the circumstances or I listen to my own doubts. This is what led to the Israelites' downfall, for they wanted Him to fight for them, and to bless them, and provide for them but only a few were prepared to take the more costly path of listening and obeying Him. That is why Jesus repeated the words of Isaiah when He said, 'You will be ever hearing but never understanding; you will be ever seeing but never perceiving. For this people's heart has become calloused; they hardly hear with their ears, and they have closed their eyes' (Matt. 13:14). But He goes on to say, 'But blessed are your eyes because they see, and your ears because they hear' (Matt. 13:16).

God Blesses us as we Hear and Obey

In his book *Does God Speak Today?*, David Pytches reports the story of what happened when an ordinary woman obeyed God with a very mundane action. She worked for a mining company in China at the time of the cultural revolution when there was widespread persecution of Christians. Part of her job was to blow a whistle each day when it was time for the miners to come up. One day, she 'heard' a voice telling her to blow the whistle now. It was far too early, so she tried to ignore it but the summons grew more and more urgent. In the end, despite the fact that it would probably get her into serious trouble, she did blow it and the miners came up. The last one was just clear of the mines when there was an earthquake. Most of the mine shafts were destroyed but not one miner was hurt. When the miners asked her what had made her whistle then, she confessed that she was a Christian and described how God had told her to whistle. Hundreds of them became Christians that day and many more after an official enquiry where she gave her testimony.[2]

It was such a simple action to blow a whistle. This wasn't hearing a long involved prophecy or a specific word of knowledge. This was a simple command to perform a simple action, an action that anyone could do. But it was as she obeyed that command that God's word was fulfilled and this wonderful miracle occurred.

Obedience is Costly

As I've thought about these stories I have been confronted over and over again with one key point, that obedience to God's word is costly. The Chinese lady obeyed at the possible cost of losing her job and even being persecuted. Jesus' relationship with His Father was overflowing with love and joy, yet His obedience meant not just His death but the reliquishment of His kingdom and glory. As it states in Philippians 2, 'Christ Jesus: Who being in very nature God, did not consider equality with God something to be grasped, but made himself nothing, taking the very nature of a servant . . . he humbled himself and became obedient to death – even death on a cross!' (Phil. 2: 5–8).

A Hard Road

Michael Ross-Watson, Itinerant Preacher and Missions Pastor at the New Life Christian Centre, in Croydon, Surrey, and his wife, Esther, knew at first hand once, just how costly obeying God's voice could be.

Michael and Esther were both training at Bible college and it was there that God called them together into marriage, at the same time giving them a joint calling to serve as missionaries in Indonesia. Their church and college leaders also felt an inner witness that this was from God, and gave them their blessing.

Thrilled at this evidence of God's leading, they joyfully set off for Indonesia. They were convinced that with God's help they would be used to evangelise in power and see this Muslim community turned around for God. The reality was very different . . .

To start with, the physical and cultural environment was overwhelmingly harsh. They'd had no preparation, no understanding of how unbearably hot and dirty it would be. The primitive living conditions, the unhygenic and dirty food and water, the lack of power, and sanitation, the cockroaches crawling out of the holes they called toilets . . . it was dreadful! It would have been easier to bear if they'd known they were having the spiritual impact they'd expected, but that too was a total loss. They'd been given no language training so had no way to communicate. The Muslim community closed ranks against them and the only time they spoke to them was when Michael and Esther were in a public place and then they would walk behind them shouting 'Infidel'.

Esther didn't even have the satisfaction of knowing she was of use in her profession of midwifery because none of the Muslim women would allow her to help them. Slowly disappointment turned to hopelessness and despair.

One day they realised they could not go on any more. They must have got it wrong. If God had truly called them, there wouldn't have been such failure and pain. They would have been able to claim God's victory instead of being overwhelmed by the difficulties. With heavy hearts they packed their bags and prepared to return home. Just before they left they had to attend a final Christian meeting and they prayed that God would give them some confirmation that they were doing the right thing in returning home.

God did speak to them, but not in the way they expected. Jeremiah 42:10 was read out and as soon as they heard the words they knew it was from God:

> If you stay in this land, I will build you up and not tear you down; I will plant you and not uproot you . . . I am with you and will save you and deliver you . . . I will show you compassion . . . However, if you say, 'We will not stay in this land,' and so disobey the Lord your God, and if you say, 'No, we will go and live in Egypt' then the sword you fear will overtake you there . . . and there you will die. (Jer. 42:10–16)

Michael and Esther felt a deep sorrow that they had been so ready to disobey God's word. They repented and unpacked their cases! They asked God to give them His love for this hostile nation.

Things did not immediately get easier but now they were determined to obey God whatever the cost. Step-by-step they made their home there. In due course they managed to learn the language and some people began to respond to God. They were eventually there for ten years, constantly struggling against the oppression and spiritual darkness. By the end of that time God had given them a true love, that was born out of their own brokenness, for both the people and the nation. He even used them to reach some high-up people and officials.

Not Always Dramatic

It won't always be the dramatic, obviously sacrificial responses that are called for. Often it will be the more mundane willingness to give up our own ideas of what we want to do or what we want to hang on to. Joanie Yoder, for example, in her book *The God Dependent Life* tells how she was cleaning the kitchen floor one day in preparation for some visitors. Half-way through the job she suddenly heard God telling her to put her coat on and go out. 'I can't go now!' she responded, 'I've got to finish this floor first.'

God said, 'Now!' 'But what will they think of me if they arrive with the floor half washed?' she moaned. It was God's next words to her that made her drop her mop and get her coat on. 'What's most important to you, to have a perfect house or to obey my word?'[3]

Not just what we do but what we are

Sometimes we can feel that so long as we are serving God and obeying those little hunches and ideas that come to us, the 'doing' things like speaking to someone, becoming a missionary, going to see somebody etc. then we are OK. But it is not just in what we do that God is calling us to obey His voice, but in what we *are*. Jesus said, 'Therefore everyone who hears these words of mine and puts them into practice is like a wise man who built his house on the rock' (Matt. 7:24).

'These words' that Jesus is referring to are all to do with our inner lives; the way we allow His love and forgiveness to transform us, the motives we have for praying and giving, the way we relate to our enemies. These aren't commands to do. These are commands to become like Him, 'to be holy because I am holy'.

When I was first a Christian and filled with the Holy Spirit, I was full of eagerness to reach people for God and impatient to see the power of God working in my life. But God never seemed to call me to do wonderful things for Him. Instead, whenever I went to church or read the Bible I kept being confronted with my need to forgive someone. But I couldn't forgive! I felt I had a right to be angry!

One day, as I was reading my Bible and praying I came to that moving passage where Jesus in His dying agony cries out 'Father forgive them, they know not what they do.' As I meditated on this I began to really see, as if for the first time, that Jesus forgave me when I was still hurting Him. He didn't wait until I was sorry, He didn't even wait until He was free of His own pain. He forgave me in the midst of incredible suffering.

Suddenly it seemed as if Jesus was whispering to me, 'You say that you can't forgive, but it's really that you won't forgive. I am the only one that can truly forgive, all I need is your "yes" and I will give you my power. Let your heart of anger become my heart of love.' I 'heard' this word deep in my heart and with God's help I did choose to forgive.

It was after I took that step of 'listening-obedience' that the door was opened in my inner life to receive a greater releasing of God's love than I'd ever known before.

I once heard the story of a lady who had also listened to God in this area. This lady had been deaf for many years and also suffered from a debilitating back condition. She was at a conference centre one night and the sermon was on forgiveness. The teacher suggested that those who needed to forgive should write down the names of people who had hurt them, forgive them, then tear the paper up. This lady was very angry and stormed out of the room. There was no way she was going to forgive yet! However, that night, God convicted her and she repented of being so hard. She did as the teacher had suggested and almost instantly experienced a deep peace. The next morning she told him what she had done and he began to pray for God to bless her. Suddenly her ears popped and sound rushed in, she had been healed of her deafness! Thrilled, the teacher began to pray for her back too. A surge of power swept down her spine and she stood up straight. Having not been able to walk without aid for many years, she now, at nearly sixty, rushed outside and did a cartwheel on the front lawn!

Joy

That cartwheel was like a symbol of the joy that springs out of our 'listening-obedience'. God promises over and over again that those who obey His Word will know joy. It is a joy that nothing else can compare with. In fact, Jesus described it as a fullness of joy, 'If you obey my commands, you will remain in my love . . . I have told you this so that my joy may be in you and that your joy may be complete' (John 15:10–11).

Or as the Amplified version of the Bible expresses it, 'I have told you these things that my joy and delight may be in you and that your joy and gladness may be full measure and complete and overflowing.'

Yes, the path may be costly and may involve real sacrifice. It may be hard to face up to our vulnerability, or our wrong or selfish attitudes. It may be that people reject or mock us as we try to do the things God has told us to do.

Yet deeper than all this, we will know the same joy that Jesus knew. 'Let us fix our eyes on Jesus, the author and perfecter of our faith, who for the joy set before Him endured the cross, scorning its shame, and sat down at the right hand of the throne of God' (Heb. 12:2).

Abraham knew that joy and as a result of his 'listening-obedience' was known as 'the friend of God'. All of us who hear Him, listen to Him and respond in loving obedience to His words, are also called the friends of God and it is to His friends that God longs to confide the deep things of His heart. 'Friendship with God is reserved for those who reverence Him. With them alone He shares the secrets of His promises . . . and when we obey Him, every path He guides us on is fragrant with His loving kindness and His truth' (Ps. 25:10, 14 [Living Bible]).

I have experienced that joy myself. It is the deep joy and awe that comes from knowing that He, the Almighty One, the Living Word, the Everlasting Father, wants to speak to me. I know there will be times when I let Him down, when I'm too busy, when I disobey . . . but in the deepest part of me I want to be a friend, who when He calls is ready to say, 'Speak, Lord, I am listening!'

Notes

Chapter 3   Listening Through His Word

1 Paul Y. Cho, *Prayer, Key to Revival* (Word, 1984), p. 44.
2 Ibid.
3 Jennifer Rees Larcombe, *Turning Point* (Hodder & Stoughton, 1994).
4 Marilyn Baker, 'Sitting At His Feet' from *By Your Side* (Nelson Word UK, 1994), © Marilyn Baker Music.

Chapter 5   Unwrapping His Gifts

1 Dennis and Rita Bennett, *The Holy Spirit and You* (Kingsway, 1971), pp. 109, 167.
2 Peter H. Lawrence, *The Hot Line* (Kingsway, 1990).
3 Harold Hill, *How to Live Like a King's Kid* (Plainfield, NJ: Logos International, 1974).

Chapter 6   Conversing with God

1 Jennifer Rees Larcombe, *Turning Point* (Hodder & Stoughton, 1994), p. 24.

Chapter 7   Creative Prayer and Intercession

1 I read about this in a publication, possibly the Lydia newsletter, but have no proof of where the story came from. Nor am I absolutely sure that it was a florist and Christian bookshop that replaced the porn shops. It was that type of beautiful thing though. I apologise for the lack of definite detail.

Chapter 8 Listening to God in Ministry and Evangelism

1 John Wimber, *Power Evangelism* (Hodder & Stoughton, 1985), p. 44.

Chapter 9 Hearing God in Today's World

1 Floyd McClung, *Living on the Devil's Doorstep* (Nelson Word, 1988).
2 Ibid. pp. 190–2.
3 Anne Long, *Listening* (Daybreak, 1990), p. 95.
4 Peter Wagner, *Signs and Wonders Today*, (Almonte Springs: Creation House, 1987) quoted in David Pytches, *Does God Speak Today?* (Hodder & Stoughton, 1989), p. 30.

Chapter 10 Handling our Mistakes

1 David Pytches, *Does God Speak Today?* (Hodder & Stoughton, 1989), p. 78.
2 Joyce Huggett, *Listening to God* (Hodder & Stoughton, 1986), p. 138.

Chapter 11 Time to Listen

1 Marilyn Baker, 'I Take Time' from *By Your Side* (Nelson Word UK, 1994), © Marilyn Baker Music.
2 Joyce Huggett, *Finding God in the Fast Lane* (Eagle, 1992), p. 93, quoted in Thomas Merton, *A Seven Day Journey with Thomas Merton* (Eagle, 1992), p. 40.
3 Joyce Huggett, *Finding God in the Fast Lane* (Eagle, 1992), p. 94.
4 Jim Borst, *Coming to God in the Stillness* (Eagle, 1992), p. 20.
5 Jean Pierre de Caussade, *The Sacrament of the Present Moment*, trans. Kitty Muggeridge (San Francisco: Harper & Row, 1982), p. xxiii.

Chapter 12 If You Love Me You Will Obey

1 A true story told by one of our team several years ago. Not her real name.

2 Peter Wagner, *Signs and Wonders Today*, (Almonte Springs: Creation House, 1987), quoted in David Pytches, *Does God Speak Today?* (Hodder & Stoughton, 1989), p. 41.

3 Joanie Yoder, *The God Dependent Life* (Hodder & Stoughton, 1991).